Knock! Knock!
A Study of the Biblical Basis of Deeper Healing

Knock! Knock!
A Study of the Biblical Basis of Deeper Healing

Published by Healing Rooms Scotland
PO Box 7010
Glasgow G76 0WF
E-mail: admin@healingrooms-scotland.com
www.healingrooms-scotland.com

Printed in the United Kingdom
ISBN 978-0-9562397-1-6

All biblical references are from the Good News Bible, unless otherwise indicated.

Acknowledgements

My heartfelt thanks go to:

Andy Fraser: (Healing Rooms, Orkney) who painstakingly edited my raw script.

Steven Anderson: (National Director Healing Rooms Scotland) for all his encouragement and endorsement of the contents of this book.

Andy Raine: (Northumbria Community) whose book "Given for Life" informed chapter 3 of this book on the concept of "motivational gifts," and his editing of that chapter.

Kayleigh Haigh: who designed the cover.

Bill: my husband, who has made space for all my enthusiasms throughout our marriage, and put up with my preoccupation with this writing.

All who agreed to have their case studies included.

TABLE OF CONTENTS:

Dedication

Gratefully dedicated to my great-grandmother, Elsie Trevanion.

I inherited and treasure her prayer-book in which she listed all her children, grand-children and great-grandchildren for whom she prayed daily—and there I am! This woman of God also wrote some beautiful poems, one of which is copied below.

"Behold I stand at the Door and knock." (Revelation 3:20)

1. Outside a Door entwined with weeds
   And tangled growth I stand.
        And as I knock,
        No answering lock,
   Is turned at My demand.
   My Hands are full of Gifts Divine
        And eager to bestow,
        I stand and wait
        Outside the gate
   So loath to turn and go.

2. Another Door I stand outside
   No clogging weeds defile.
        A welcome sweet
        My knock doth greet
   'Tis opened with a smile.
        With hands outspread
        I blessings shed
   As on My way I go.

And Heaven's light
Puts gloom to flight
When heart My peace doth know.

3. My peace I give, not as the world
   Elusive gives to you,
   But Heaven's own joy
   Without alloy
   Springs up on earth for you.
   The valleys stand so thick with corn
   The pools so full of rain,
   That Baca's vale
   Is made a well
   And echoes Heaven's refrain.

4. And when at last thy work is done
   And evening shadows come,
   My rod and staff
   Will comfort give,
   My Light will lead thee Home.
   Then, in the stillness of the dawn
   When calm rests over all,
   I'll knock once more
   On the closed door
   And, one more soul is born.

Elsie Trevanion 12th October 1911

Foreword

God our Father has such wonderful purposes for our lives, and views each one of us from a standpoint that sees the incredible potential within us. He longs to be gracious to us and bring us into a greater experience of life in all its fullness that Jesus came to impart (*John 10:10*). Yet so many people have been robbed, damaged and crushed.

The book of Proverbs tells us that two main things crush our spirits, dampening our lives and restricting our potential. These are heartache *(Proverbs 15:13)* and a deceitful tongue (*Proverbs 15:4*). All of us experience some degree of wounding, hurt, pain, trauma and loss throughout our lifetimes, and sadly some people experience a great deal of this. That can all be bad enough, but often on top of such heartache come lies and deceit that bring a further crushing to our spirits and trap us into the effects of these painful experiences.

The all too common pains of abuse and rejection do not come alone but bring with them the lies of worthlessness, devaluing us and grossly colouring our vision of who we really are in Christ. Alongside comes the debilitating power of fear which silently dominates many lives.

However there is good news because there is a Healer – the Son of God, Jesus – who redeems and rescues us, forgives and frees us, and restores our souls. He comes full of grace to forgive and heal the heartache, and full of truth to dissolve the power of deceit.

Over many years of being involved, often by sheer necessity, in what might be referred to as 'inner healing' prayer, we have witnessed time and again the wonderful grace of God break through into tormented and tortured souls bringing glorious light and life. Being involved in such work is one of the most awesome privileges this life offers.

In this book Kirsten Coulter writes from her own experiences of God's healing in her life and in the lives of many others she has prayed with over her long years of ministry. Kirsten skillfully interweaves teaching, testimony and biblical case studies in this dynamic little book. The ministry guidelines are very helpful and throughout the pages you will discover some great nuggets of wisdom.

If you have areas of deep wounding in your life then know there is hope and there is a Healer. Find His love, grace and truth. Find help if you need it, but don't live out your days trapped by the pain of the past when there is a life of greater purpose and joy that God longs to introduce you to.

If you have a desire to bring such healing to others then pursue this wonderful work. Read this book and others like it, get equipped, find those you can learn from and partner with in following Jesus by bringing 'freedom for the prisoners and release to the oppressed.'

Steven Anderson
National Director, Healing Rooms Scotland

A personal note: A Passion for Healing

"Why are you so passionate about healing?" The question recently came from one of my superiors in the church, and it has focussed my thoughts. Here are four reasons:

1. The Gospel: It is the primary message of Good News:

> *"Jesus went all over Galilee, teaching in the synagogues, preaching the Good News about the Kingdom, and healing people who had all kinds of disease and sickness." (Matthew 4:23)*

2. Jesus' Ministry: The majority of what is recorded is about healing. Healing authenticates His claims to be the Messiah:

> *"Go back and tell John what you are hearing and seeing: the lame can walk, those who suffer from dreaded skin diseases are made clean, the deaf hear, and the dead are brought back to life, and the Good News is preached to the poor. Happy are those who have no doubts about Me!" (Matthew 11:4, 5)*

3. **My own experience**: I have been healed of so much over a long period of time.

4. **Everyone needs healing**:

"Jesus answered him: I am the way, the Truth and the Life." (John 14:6). Ill health of body, mind and spirit is a legacy of the rebellion of mankind against God. What is salvation? Certainly it is not just a ticket to heaven. One of the New Testament Greek words for the verb "to save" is "*sozo*" which means "wholeness".

Jesus came to die on the cross to save us from the consequences of our turning away from our Creator, who intended us to live a life free from bodily sickness, mental stress and guilt, here and now. We are damaged goods and we need repairing. I believe in life before death as well as after it!

Introduction

"That was wonderful—but where is your scriptural basis?" The speaker was a young and eager Youth With A Mission student. She had come with me to assist in a week's camp for young people from the school in Livingston where I taught Religious Education. For some years I had been practicing "inner healing".

The person we were praying for had deep fears rooted in her past which had been brought to the surface by the location and décor of the Outdoor Education hostel where we were staying. It was very isolated, situated near Ben More in Argyll, and when we arrived the walls were covered in murals depicting ugly, threatening and devilish images, which some unenlightened previous group had been allowed to paint on.

As soon as possible, we covered these with paintings of scenes from the Bible, crosses and other Christian images, and then we had a lively time of praise and prayer for cleansing of the building. But the legacy remained in the child's mind.

After we had discerned the root of the fears, we prayed for the little girl, introduced her to Jesus, and the transformation in her whole outlook was immediate and amazing.

At that stage, in the late 1970's, I had never read anything on the subject, and had never been to any training sessions. I do not know if they even existed. I had been baptized in the Holy Spirit, I was totally taught by Him in what I was doing. I just listened and obeyed, and the Lord graciously allowed me to see sometimes quite spectacular changes in people's lives.

But, of course, the young student was quite right, and I began to search the scriptures for evidence that my insight and the way I was ministering was part of the Kingdom message, and especially looking to see if Jesus specifically addressed the healing of memories.

This book has been in formation since then. I have appended guidance for ministry notes at the end of each section, but this is not meant to be prescriptive. This is not a handbook of methods, for God has no set methods. He tailors his work of healing to the individual, their need and their understanding. Each person is unique; with every person he or she prays for, the minister of healing needs the continuous and specific guidance of the Holy Spirit.

I offer some of the biblical basis for Jesus' wonderful work of healing the inner person—a process which goes on all our lives—as we shall see.

Kirsten Coulter

Chapter 1
Who's there?

"In my Father's house are many mansions."
(John 14:2 A.V.)

A young woman, who I know has many problems in her life, came into my home for the first time a few weeks ago. She sat down in my living-room, and accepted a cup of tea but was clearly ill at ease at first. However, after a time she remarked: "This is such a peaceful room". I had just been playing some Christian music, and it is a room which has witnessed much Spirit-filled worship, spiritual dance and prayer, both individual and corporate. Our homes need to be places where people meet Jesus, even if they don't recognise it.

What are the *"mansions"* that Jesus talked about? This text is often used at funerals. It is recognised that Jesus is talking about eternal life. He goes on to say: "I go to prepare a place for you—I will come back and take you to be with me, that you also may be where I am." It is assumed that there are lots of big houses in heaven, beyond the grave, that we, as believers, will be privileged to live in. That could be so, but I would like to suggest another way of understanding what He meant.

"Mansions" in this context can be variously translated. The Greek word, *"monai"*, is a room or an abode, a staying place, not necessarily different compartments in heaven, but sometimes understood to be a resting-place

along the road, a welcome break in the long, tedious journey.

John's Gospel depicts eternal life not just as a goal we reach beyond the grave, but a life, His life, starting here and now. I would suggest that Jesus could be indicating that we are the "*mansions*". We are called to be His resting-place, where the weary traveller finds peace. But so many people are not at peace, there are deep underlying disturbances in our lives.

Knock! Knock! Who's there?
"Behold I stand at the door and knock." (Revelation 3:20 A.V.)

We often refer, perfectly legitimately, to *Revelation 3:20* when we are leading a person to Christ for the first time. We say that Jesus wants to come into our lives and change us, clean us up, bring us peace, "*eat together with us*", just as if He was one of the family. Friendships and confidences are shared around the family meal table. We say Jesus is standing outside the door, depicted in the Holbein painting as a front door without a handle on the outside and that He is a gentleman, and will not force His way in. He is waiting for us to open the door from the inside and welcome Him in.

We go on to point out that He says: *"If anyone hears My voice and opens the door, I **will** come in."* Not 'if you're good enough I might', or 'if you're clever enough and understand all about the Bible and Jesus'—and so on. No! He says "*I will.*" So the hearer opens the door of his life and is challenged to believe that, having done so, Jesus keeps His promise and is within. At some point soon after that, the hearer demonstrates by a changed life that this event has indeed happened.

As with so many scriptures that are familiar we limit the scope. In this one we conclude that Jesus has come into our lives – so the goal is reached. But actually John the divine, in Revelation, was writing and rebuking an existing church, in this case the church at Laodicea, of whom he says the Lord's observations to the angel of the church were:*" lukewarm… neither hot nor cold, I will spit you out of my mouth. You say: 'I am rich; I have acquired wealth; I don't need a thing', but you do not realise that you are wretched, miserable, poor, blind and naked."* (Revelation 3: 16, 17.L.B.)

The Revelation churches are models of churches, made up of the people of God who have come to know Jesus, down through the ages, and I would venture to suggest Laodicea is very typical of many of our modern western churches and of the individual Christians within them. We have lost our way, our cutting-edge, our hot zeal for truth and service to Jesus. The Lord is asking us to repent, to turn round, to rediscover where our true riches are in His life. We have lost sight of them under a pile of trivia which we use to try to satisfy our cravings for meaning and joy in life.

So this text is not just for new Christians, to assure them they have arrived. It is only a beginning place. It is for us! It is a fresh challenge. I explain to new Christians, especially to children, that it is as if we have a house inside us (an abode — a mansion?) and when we let Jesus into our lives, He comes through the front door into the hallway, where all the obvious things that are wrong in our lives are exposed for Him to see and clean up, polish and make like new. All the things that have been part of the conviction of sin and need are immediately addressed and the person feels new and clean inside. Wonderful!

Then, sometime later - days, weeks or months - Jesus starts knocking on another door inside our mansions: the dining-room possibly. "Can I come in here?" He asks. He wants to share His food with us in a clean and welcoming place. He wants to enter and clean that room up too. If we open the door, He may intrude upon personal space, maybe sort out priorities, but as a result, we experience unimaginable companionship and wonderful feeding for our spirits.

That done, He moves on — to the kitchen. This is where our ideas are "cooked up" perhaps. Where food, tools, gadgets and household items enter the house of our souls in our shopping-bags. Some of these are necessary and wholesome, but some are not at all helpful.

He maybe sometime later enters the living-room. This is where we are entertained and entertain. It is a warm, secure and welcoming place we hope.
However, we may have polluted it with unsavoury entertainment, filling our minds with dirty material affecting our peace and cluttering our lives so much that

there is no room for other people. He may mess up what we treasure as our social life, but He replaces it with real, open friendships and wonderful, deep laughter.

The bathroom - He is not just interested in our souls, He wants to clean up our bodies too, our appearance and the way we dress ourselves, to be fit temples of the Holy Spirit. We sometimes, like small boys, don't want to wash the tide-line off our necks, and our bad habits are smelly and off-putting! The clothes we wear and the way we present ourselves need not be expensive and they can reflect our personalities and age-group in fashions, styles and colours. But we should still be clean and well-groomed. Our heritage is to be princes and princesses in this heavenly kingdom, and we should look like it!

This mansion has hundreds of rooms: it will take a life-time and more to clear them all out! Eventually He gets to the basement where all kinds of secrets lie - rubbish that has been discarded, but hoarded "in case it may come in useful". It is musty with damp and mildewed and has affected the atmosphere of the whole house, and much needs breaking up, recycling, or actually discarding, taking to the dump, then forgotten .

Finally, He climbs the ladder to the attic hatch and knocks. In here hidden symbols lie buried under dust, and have never seen the light of day for years - our most painful memories recorded in faded photographs, discarded toys and ornaments. He wants to enter through the hatch and search these out that they may be confronted, freshened and made pleasant and easy to live with.

It is often the attic that Jesus wants to address in this book. He wants our "mansions" to be clean, peaceful, devoid of clutter, open and free.

He has a right to take others, such as ourselves, who have been made as containers for the riches of His glory, whether we are Jews or Gentiles, and to be kind to us so that everyone can see how very great His glory is. (Romans 9: 23, 24 L.B.)

When we gave our lives to Jesus, we gave Him permission to sort us out, so we cannot complain when He does so. We are greatly privileged to be chosen by Him and we should welcome any chance we have to make our presentation of Him more attractive. That is what healing of the inner person does - and it shows on the outside!

Chapter 2
God the Father and the Mother

"Our Father in heaven." (Matthew 6:9)

The word of knowledge had been a picture of a sailing-boat skimming across the water. The troubled young woman gave a start and cried out: "He wanted a boy—and what he got was me" She was an only child, so her father made her into a tom-boy. He certainly took her out and entertained her. She enjoyed these trips and his one-to-one his attention, but it was always male-orientated activities, and inside this teenager was a young woman trying to find her feminine nature. Deep in her heart she interpreted these activities, rightly or wrongly, as rejection.

"Some, however, did receive Him and believed in Him; so He gave them the right to become God's children." (John 1:12.) All the relationships that we foster on earth are not just intended to be ends in themselves. They are ordained by God to reflect the quality of our relationship with Him, expressed both corporately and individually in our life-times. Jesus taught us to call God "Father". He created and nurtures the whole of creation, but especially human beings who were made in His image. The human race lost that spiritual sonship at the Fall when they rebelled against the authority of God who set the parameters of behaviour Himself, as a caring responsible parent only in our best interests.

But it is more complex than that because we assume that God is male - designated only as Father. But the scriptures prove beyond doubt that He is neither exclusively male nor female: He is both. God is our heavenly Mother as well as our Father. God gave us two parents who complement each other, and reflect His nature. *"So God created humankind in His image; in the image of God He created him; male and female He created them." (Genesis 1:27 N.R.S.V.)*

The tenderness of the Mother God is reflected in Scripture: *"Can a woman forget her nursing child, or show no compassion on the son of her womb? Even these may forget, yet I will not forget you."*
(Isaiah 49: 15.N.R.S.V.)
"He shall cover you with His feathers and under His wings you will find refuge." (Psalm 91:4 N.I.V.)

So it is not just a Father/ Son relationship we need to explore, but a parent/ child relationship too. The designation Father and the male pronouns are simply convenient shorthand to express that relationship. The Parent/child relationship was restored in Jesus the Son of God, and He conferred that privilege on all who believed and received Him. That privilege is expressed in that we are able to call the Almighty God *"Abba"* meaning *"Daddy"*. *(Romans 8:15)* It expresses the intimacy He seeks for us, the immense love He has for us. He loves us as much as He loves His own Son who was sinless!

He is love. The aim of our whole life is to discover the quality of that love. We all need a revelation of this truth. Paul expresses this in his letter to the Ephesian church:

"I pray that you may have your roots and foundation in love, so that you, together with all of God's people, may have the power to understand how broad and long, how high and deep, is Christ's love." (Ephesians 3:17b, 18)

But deep in all of us are barriers to this knowledge. "You stupid child—now they will all have to be re-laid and it will cost the earth." On and on my mother went. She was justifiably angry, but the worst of it was that all I was trying to do was give her a nice surprise but it had back-fired. It was an apparently trivial incident when I was nine years old, but it rankled in my mind for many years.

My parents had a new house built to their specifications opposite the school where my father had recently taken the post of headmaster. The house was almost complete, it was decorated and the workmen had just laid a Marley tile floor. We went to admire the house, and my parents had to make quick visit to the local solicitor just to complete some paper-work so that we could move in very shortly.

Left on my own, I surveyed the tiles. They were grubby where the partly dried tile cement had oozed over them and where the workmen had trampled in muddy boots. I can remember thinking how pleased my mother would be if I cleaned the floor as a surprise for her return. So I found a bucket and a mop and sloshed about happily. My mother walked in on this scene, and hit the roof! My efforts had softened the cement and dislodged some of the tiles. The whole floor had to be re-laid. My mother's fury, her disgust and her disparaging comments bruised my affectionate heart and persisted into adulthood.

Many years later I recognised that I was in the bondage of continuing desire for her approval. It didn't always inhibit me. I still made my own choices flying in the face of her discouragement real or imaginary, but it caused pain and tension within me. I took Jesus into that house and amongst the ruined tiles I forgave my mother who was justifiably angry but who really didn't know what she was doing when she gave me such a telling off.

Parents often inflict damage on their children quite unwittingly. We are designed to want to please our parents. They are our most important mentors, our most severe critics and our greatest admirers. I can remember the positive effect of my mother's enormous efforts to be present when ever I was taking part in sports games, competitions, dramatic productions or local festival events. She was usually working some way away, and would sacrificially take time off just to be there and watch me scrape through to the final moment in the high jump competition. She would also make every effort to nurse me through various childhood illnesses, even if she had to take unpaid leave.

But, like most parents it is thoughtlessness which creates the scenario to become the negative and painful memory. As tiny children our parents have the power of God to us: we are totally dependent on their provision, their approval, their protection and care. Our fathers and mothers together are set to be the model of what God is like, and this takes root in our psyche. So when we encounter God the Father and Mother, this image can often obscure our understanding of parenthood, leave a distorted legacy and deeply affect our relationship with Him.

God chose our parents ideally to complement one another in the full realization of their personalities, because all of us are a mixture of male and female characteristics. We are socially taught to expect our father to be the authority figure and the disciplinarian, and our mother to have the gentler, nurturing approach. We also expect women to be the weaker, dependent sex. The Scripture describes the church as the Bride of Christ, an image of purity, obedience, dependency and the one who responds to the advances of the Bridegroom.

But Jesus Himself lived in human flesh, having laid aside the privileges of divinity, and dependent upon the Holy Spirit to guide Him - yet He was not weak - He demonstrated that to lean on our heavenly Father for everything makes us fully human, and victorious in life.

The inclusion in our understanding that God is our Mother, reminds us that we have an intimate, exclusive bond with Her. We came from the heart of Her being - the womb, and were connected by an umbilical cord which nourished us directly when we were helpless and totally dependent and not in a fit state to earn such care. It is a symbol of unearned, unconditional grace and provision. She has the rights of ownership and the tie of creation.

We respond in love to our mothers by embrace, acceptance and appreciation of her provision. We confide in her, assume her support, her life-long friendship, and recognise something of ourselves in her. We want to please her and protect her. Sometimes we cannot break that cord, sometimes our mothers cannot let go, to the detriment of our marriages. We are to honour our parents but grow to be responsible adults. God the perfect parent teaches us how to come to maturity in Him.

Often people choose as their partner someone who fills in the character traits they lack. But, of course, parents are human beings. They make mistakes in the choice of mate and most have their own problems and legacies of poor parenting to cope with. Even the best of us have usually made mistakes unintentionally, have been insensitive or have sought our own interests before those of our offspring.

Our human fathers or their substitutes in male role models, or our mothers or their female role models may have been abusive, overly strict and frightening, dominant, demeaning or unrealistically demanding in their attitudes to us. Or they could have been over-indulgent, weak and indecisive, breaking promises either in regard to stated rules of discipline or in their promises of treats. In some cases they are simply absent.

Incidentally too, this is why it is dangerous to endorse the adoption model of gay and lesbian couples. Adoptive parents of the same sex present a distorted and unbalanced image of God to the young child, making it more difficult to relate to Him as a parent.

"The son who will receive his father's property is treated just like a slave while he is young, even though he really owns everything. While he is young, there are men who take care of him and manage his affairs until the time set by his father. In the same way, we too were slaves of the ruling spirits of the universe before we reach spiritual maturity. But when the right time finally came, God sent His own Son. He came as the son of a human mother and lived under the Jewish law, to redeem those who were under the law, so that we might become God's sons. To show that you are His sons, God sent the Spirit of His Son into our hearts, the Spirit who cries out "Father my Father". So then you are no longer a slave but a son. And since you are His son, God will give you all He has for His sons." (Galatians 4:1-6)

While we are still unhealed we find it hard to "come of age" in relation to our heavenly Father and receive the legacy of His life in us, and understand our glorious sonship. If our fathers were tough with us, we fear God; if they were overly soft, we think we can get away with anything with God. We are "slaves" to the wrong images of parenthood.

Our painful experiences tell us that parental figures let us down. The damaged inner person says: "If I disobey Him, He will reject me" or "I can only rely on Him up to a point, when there's a crisis, He'll fail me." We need to reach a place where our mind and hearts agrees with the Word of God: Our Heavenly Father is to be trusted in all circumstances—even when I've blown it! *"Perfect love drives out all fear" (1 John 4:18b)*

Perfect love contains the paradox of interdependence. The Trinity reveals the need for love to have an object and a response. God's nature is to love, and, amazingly, He has made Himself vulnerable to us. He needs our love to make love complete. There is no hierarchy in the Godhead: Their relationship of Father, Son and Holy Spirit is expressed in their perfect harmony as they work together. Rather than a triangle of relationship, they move in a circle. As children of God we are included in that circle, so become full-partners in bringing about the kingdom of God on earth. That is mind-boggling! It underlines the value God puts on us as part of His family. Even if we don't fully trust Him---He trusts us!

Spare the Rod
"My son, pay attention when the Lord corrects you, and do not be discouraged when He rebukes you. Because the Lord corrects everyone He loves. Because the Lord corrects everyone He loves and punishes everyone He accepts as a son." (Hebrews 12: 5, 6)

Because of a wrong image of Him, we so often misunderstand when God disciplines us. Our earthly parents may display attitudes which fuel their approach to discipline.

27

1. **Moodiness**: A very human trait, as we are subject to our emotions. God's mood is constant. His love knows no boundaries.

2. **Injustice**: Our parents do not understand our motives in all we do or see - all the factors in the situation.
   God knows all. The Lord said to him--- "*I do not judge as man judges. Man looks at the outward appearance, but I look upon the <u>heart</u>.*" *(1 Samuel 16:7c)*

3. **Unreasonableness**: Our earthly parents may react out of anger, frustration or fear, however God always listens to us; He recognises mis-understandings and assesses accurately.

4. **Embarrassment:** We let our parents down by our behaviour. They are often more afraid of what others will think. God is concerned only for His holy Name (*Isaiah 48:9*). We bear His name, but He can take care of that Himself!

5. **Pride:** Our parents recognise that their bad parenting may have been a large factor in our misbehaviour. God is the perfect Father. He has no fear of failure.

6. **Stress**: Our parents may be distraught and overburdened with other issues and strains, not least in their relationship with each other. Maybe they just want us out of their sight and for a time. God is always there for us, His patience is inexhaustible and He is not distracted!

7. **Vindictiveness**: Some parents take out their frustrations on their children, as the weaker objects of both physical and verbal abuse.

God is always merciful: *"He knows what we are made of; He remembers that we are but dust." (Psalm 103:14)*
All He wants to do is to protect us from the consequences of our own foolishness!

Does God punish us?
"If you don't punish your son, you don't love him." (Proverbs 13:24a)

One bright summer's night, when I was about nine years old, I stayed out and played in the park opposite my house, ignoring my parents' call that it was time for bed, and hiding when they appeared. When, at about 10.30pm, I decided I'd better go in, I found my mother beside herself with worry and furious with me. She sent me to bed without any supper. I can remember lying there awake, waiting for my father who I knew would not let me down. Eventually, the door slid quietly open and he appeared, finger to his lips. He was carrying a glass of milk, two biscuits and an apple. My father was a gentle, mild-tempered man, and I know I was positively spoilt by him. This coloured my view of God the Father, but He was not about to let me get away with disobedience!

For many of us the concept of "tough love" is a novel idea. Many Christians are brought up on the image of "Gentle Jesus meek and mild."
"I am the first and the last, the beginning and the end." (Revelation 21:6b)
God is holy so He is committed to fight sin and evil. He loves us and wants the best for us, so we can trust any corrective measures. A good father prevents his child

from putting their finger in the fire. If we have asked God to be our Father we cannot complain when He answers the prayer! We have given Him the right to choose our path for us. He knows the end from the beginning. His way may be difficult and painful for a time, and we might have the tendency to see this as rejection. The faster we run back to God, however, the quicker the problem is over.

"All right," the Lord said to Satan, "everything he has is in your power, but you must not hurt Job himself." (Job 1:12)

"The Lord God asked the woman, 'Why did you do this?' She replied, "The snake tricked me into eating it."' (Genesis 3:13)

We have a tendency when things go wrong to behave like children blaming their siblings. We blame it all on satanic forces and say we are "under attack". That may be so at times, but I prefer to see Satan as "God's sheepdog" snapping at our heels, manoeuvring us into the best position for us. The sheepdog is never unleashed! God has infinite patience, but patience must have a limit or it becomes indulgence.

Maturity is recognizing that God allows us to push the boundaries until it violates the purposes of His kingdom and then He intervenes. If our greatest desire is to see His Kingdom come on earth, we can only concur. When we meet Him face to face at the judgement seat of heaven, we will find that in His mercy He has provided an Advocate for us, Jesus Christ, who will plead our case - a further extension of His patience.

Family relationships

Again these may be distorted by our experience. The children in His family do not need to worry about who is getting the most attention. He loves each one of us equally but differently, enjoying each individual personality He created. He has no specific favourites, because we are all His favourites! He concentrates His whole attention on each one of us all the time. He can do that: He is God who is not limited in time and space.

Jealousy is one of the most destructive forces in the Christian family. Once we realise how much He values and cherishes each individual child of His, then we know He delights in us, just as much as He does His only begotten Son, Jesus. Those in the church can become, at best, our new family. These are not mere satellites circulating around our ego, or just good friends. They become intimate companions, bound together in the interdependent circle of God's love.

Relationships which include a spiritual dimension are bound to be on a deeper level even than blood ties. We see in the New Testament the new believers relied upon each other in every way - financial, practical, emotional and spiritual - their lives were bound up with each other. How we have lost this aspect in our western church life! Mostly, as church people, we live in our own social and material bubble and only superficially brush shoulders with our brothers and sisters in Christ at the church services or meetings. We need to restore the church to be a healing environment, where each person is accepted as they are.

We were made to be a part of a family and so many have little understanding of the commitment of family life. They may have lost contact with, been bereaved, or be disappointed in their relationship with brothers, sisters, sons, daughters, cousins and so on. Our attitudes and practical care, our availability, the understanding that our love can be taken for granted, just as we assume our family's love would be, can be a powerful part of the healing process in them. This may takes years of commitment in patient care, taking the person through stages of the development of their personality. We may feel that this is not our gifting or calling and realise that someone else might do a much better job. We must be prepared to let go as well.

Triggers to memory
"I don't like him, and I don't want him to come back". The speaker was a person who had dementia, and it was about a volunteer befriender who had a gentle personality and was well-liked by all his other clients. Eventually we discovered that the befriender reminded this gentleman of a social worker, a professional colleague who had let him down on several occasions.

As we minister to damaged people we need to be alert to patterns of response. Often, irrationally, a wounded person will recoil from another person, without knowing them well and without good reason. If we take time to trace this back, we can discover that in their past there has been a similar person either in looks or personality. We see in this case it brought back a memory of a painful experience. This can be a useful tool in understanding their difficulty, and often the trigger leads to a flaw in the parent/child relationship. *"My father and mother may abandon me, but the Lord will take care of me." (Psalm 27:10)*

We usually have in a prayer team a man and a woman. In my experience we often reflect the male or female aspect of God to the hurting person; we stand in those particular gaps. So it is helpful when we recognise a breakdown in a relationship, for example with a father, to suggest that the male in the team prays initially for the person, as the male image and voice conveys healing on a very deep level, especially if a prophetic word is spoken - a word of knowledge or wisdom. Also, with permission, for example, a male hug after ministry would help seal the reassurance for the hurting person. And this could be so with other relationships - mother, grand-mother, grandfather, brother, sister, friend and so on.

This aspect of deeper healing is so significant. For myself, when such a situation is revealed by the Holy Spirit and recognised by the hurting person, I always have perfect faith in the process of healing. God is committed to having a deep relationship with His twice-born children, He wants friends He can share His life with, and will do anything that will facilitate that and remove the barriers we raise because of our traumatic past.

Jacob: fathered by God
Genesis 25:19-26

Jacob's name means 'heel' or 'usurper'. He emerged from his mother's womb hanging onto his brother's heel, as if he were trying to drag him back. Rebecca, Isaac's wife, was about to give birth to twins. She was told by God that the two nations that would descend from her sons would be forever at war with each other. Their respective characters seemed shaped from birth.

Esau was born first - covered in red hair. He was the tough guy of the two and would be expected to dominate his more delicate brother. He grew up to be a hunter, a lover of the outdoor life. As the boys grew up, their parents exacerbated their differences by making favourites. Isaac, like Esau, loved fresh meat so favoured this elder brother. Rebecca gave all her attention to Jacob. She mollycoddled him, and took his side in disputes.

Jacob was a schemer and noted his brother's excessive appetites. He waited until Esau came in very hungry from hunting, and sharpened the hunger by ensuring that his brother smelled the savoury, red bean stew he had been cooking. Esau could not wait to satisfy his hunger, and Jacob used the stew as a bribe. He persuaded Esau to sell him his rights as the first-born son. Esau demonstrated that his greed was more important than his heritage. He became the epitome of a people who were always ready to put material gain and fleshly appetites before spiritual values. The Edomites, his descendants, became a constant hindrance to the Israelites, Jacob's descendants.

Genesis 27
Jacob lived much of his life by his wits, at first imitating his dominant mother, who was the arch-schemer. When Isaac was old, blind and frail, and, possibly, somewhat senile, but ready to pass on his responsibilities as patriarch to his eldest son, Esau, Rebecca was ready to frustrate this plan. She made sure that Esau was out of the way, hunting for the savoury meat his father loved. She then prepared some meat, covered Jacob's arms with animal hair, put some of Esau's clothes on him which smelled of the outdoors, and sent him in to his father to claim the blessing of the first-born in his brother's place. Jacob fell in with this plan. It seems he was weak and easily led. Rebecca already knew that God had foretold the brother's destiny, nothing could frustrate God's purposes, but her indulgence of Jacob made her make sure of this.

Her plan was successful, and Jacob received the blessing ahead of Esau. But the outcome was, at first, not to his advantage. He became an outlaw because of his brother's desire for revenge. Worse still, it distorted his character: he had learned to get on in life by cheating. However, God does not make mistakes. He knew all about Jacob and he saw and valued the hidden inner person. He foresaw what he would become. It was to be a long and painful process of redemption.

Genesis 28
First he had to meet his God. As he fled from Esau's wrath, he settled down to sleep in a "holy" place. In the presence of God, he saw a *"stairway to heaven,"* with angels moving up and down on it. The Lord stood beside him, and promised him numerous descendants and the land where he lay as his inheritance. Jacob had grown up believing that the world owed him a living. He did not seem to realise that he had no claims upon God's favour. He was afraid but still tried to bargain with God.

Genesis 28: 20
He demanded God's protection, His provision, and a safe return to his father's home. Then - very big of him - he would give the Lord a tenth of all that God had provided. In spite of his amazing experience of the grace of God, he had a long way to go before he understood what it was to be a disciple! But God had someone in mind who would be Jacob's match in counter-deception.

Genesis 29
God ensured that Jacob was put into the hands of his uncle Laban who perceived Jacob's naivety, and made use of it. Jacob had fallen in love with his beautiful and shapely cousin Rachel, Laban's younger daughter. Laban persuaded him to work for him for seven years to earn her hand in marriage. After the seven years were up, Jacob claimed his bride. But in the dark of the wedding night Laban swapped the bride, his oldest daughter, Leah, who is described as having *"weak eyes",* and evidently had no claim to beauty.

Jacob did not discover the deception until after the wedding-night was over, but could not stand up to his uncle's scheming. Laban offered him Rachel, as well, as his wife, as long as he worked another seven years for him. Jacob was foolish enough to agree. At first his hopes and dreams for Rachel were frustrated, because it is only Leah and two slave girls belonging to his wives who gave him sons. Rachel remained barren for a long time, until she finally gave him his eleventh son, Joseph. Jacob had by now become more wise to his uncle's scheming. He decided to leave and return home. Before this, he knew that he could not trust his uncle to stick to any agreement over wages; he had changed these ten times during his stay. So he made a bargain with Laban. He would continue to take care of Laban's flocks, but that he would separate the flocks and herds by isolating the black sheep and the spotted or speckled goats. These he would take for himself, and leave the others for Laban.

Laban agreed but made sure that these animals were spirited away before Jacob could claim them. Jacob, undeterred, managed to make sure that the animals in his charge bred spotted and speckled offspring. He also managed to make sure that his animals were stronger than the ones identified as Laban's. He had outwitted his protagonist: he was still Jacob the 'usurper'.

Once God has got hold of us, He does not let go until he reshapes our attitudes and He uses all kinds of situations to bring about our healing. Like all of us, Jacob had to face his past, repent and put right his offences and seek forgiveness. He returned to Canaan, but was dreading his meeting with his estranged brother, Esau. He desired to be reconciled, and seek forgiveness, but possibly his motives were not entirely pure. Maybe his concern was still largely for his own preservation. He fretted and schemed, and then devised the idea of sending gifts ahead of him to soften his brother's attitude. He also arranged the travelling order of his family, making sure that his favourite wife, Rachel and her son were in the rear of the caravan in case Esau attacked.

Perhaps because of his fear, Jacob withdrew and went to a solitary place, and there he at last met his God face to face. We are told that he wrestled with 'a man', until daybreak. He prevailed but in the fight his hip was put out of joint, and he retained a permanent limp, a symbol of his weakness and dependence upon God. For Jacob recognised the man as being the Lord and demonstrated his determination to hold on to Him. Jacob vowed he would not let him go until He blessed him. The Lord changed his name to 'Israel', after whom the people of God were named, and He blessed him.

Jacob exclaimed, "I have seen God face to face, and lived." The Jews believed that the holiness of God would destroy them if they so much as looked upon Him. Jacob had made some progress towards emotional and spiritual maturity, but he was committed to serve God instead of his own interests. God preserved him and he found his brother received him and had forgiven him.

Genesis 35

Jacob was now obedient and submissive to God who told him to 'return to Bethel', where He had first met Jacob when he was running away from Esau all those years ago. He instructed his family to destroy all symbols of their worship of foreign gods. He built an altar and declared his loyalty to the "*God who helped me in my time of trouble and who has been with me everywhere I have gone.*" *(Genesis 35: 3b)*

He is required to return "to his first love", and in so doing he renews his relationship with his heavenly Father, hears again the blessings of grace and erects a memorial stone which he consecrates to the Lord. His understanding of fatherhood has undergone a transformation. He recognises, through the discipline that God has imposed on him, that he cannot manipulate circumstances and people to get his own way. Jacob the 'usurper' has now been usurped by his Lord.

Unfortunately this now gentle and mild-mannered old man has not learned the lessons of the legacy of indulgent parenthood - as we will see in chapter 6, when he is about to spoil his son, Joseph, and perpetuate that weakness onto the next generation.

Notes: Ministry

When taking part in prayer ministry:

1. Take notice and listen to the prompt in your mind which says "father" or "mother" or indicates another significant relationship.

2. Be bold to relate an image, a picture or a word of knowledge that comes to you, however bizarre it seems.

3. Note: A 'word of knowledge' or a 'word of wisdom' can come in the form of a scriptural quote or reference, it can come as a word or a sentence, or as a picture or description. Sometimes it comes beforehand, sometimes as the person speaks and often when we begin to pray for them. The person ministering may have no idea what the 'word' refers to; they have received it from the Spirit of God. (See Chapter 13 on the 'rhema' word of God.)

4. It may be that when the person is telling their story they may, without knowing, refer to a relevant incident or object. This can then be followed up. This insight must be carefully explored with the person. We can get it wrong! It is best to approach the subject with a tentative question e.g. "Does this scripture/ picture/ object mean anything to you?" If the answer is "No", then drop the subject, it may be that the word or image is symbolic of their situation rather than literal, and needs a little unpacking, but don't labour it! Sometimes the person will make the connection later - even

weeks later. If, however, the word "hits the nail on the head", there and then, it is a great encouragement to faith for both the person and the minister!

5. As the person tells his or her story, look for patterns of behaviour especially in relationships. Listen for attitudes, especially to the ones questioning God's goodness. They may well indicate an unhappy past relationship with significant adults. These indicators could be the key to the hurting person's problems. But take a gentle approach using a question form: "Does this mean anything to you?" Don't probe too hard if the person shows any sign of backing off. They may not be ready to face the pain of their past just yet. You may be only a link in the chain of self-awareness. Remember that God may be doing a long-term, patient work in the person's life. It may be enough that you have demonstrated that God knows and cares.

6. Be ready and aware that you may become the incarnation of God the Father's or Mother's love. In relating to you as a parent they may receive some understanding of the love of God.

Chapter 3
Nature or Nurture?

"I'm a practical man. I like to make sure things run smoothly, and besides, I couldn't stand up and preach." The man who said this may or may not have been making an excuse. We have the example of Stephen in the Acts of the Apostles, who started out being appointed as one in charge of practical matters in the church- as a deacon, one who served - so the apostles could get on with their job of spiritual leadership. Stephen, who is full of the Holy Spirit, does the job assigned to him, but is also found performing miracles. He ends up not only giving one of the longest sermons recorded in the New Testament, but also being the first martyr, and before his death sees visions of Jesus and God, and prays out loud for the forgiveness of his persecutors.

It is possible that Stephen's gifts may have been misunderstood by those who appointed him; maybe the supernatural power of the Holy Spirit within him just had to manifest itself. God does not allow us to label people and put them in boxes which restrict the realization of His work in them.

However, we all of us start with raw genetic material which shows itself in our natural traits of character. There have been many attempts through history to categorise human personality, some more detailed than others. These all have the same aim, not to lock us into a pattern of responses nor to excuse bad behaviour, but simply to recognise our unique qualities and weaknesses. "*We are to use our different gifts, in accordance with the grace God has given us." (Romans 12:6a)*

The list of gifts in Romans 12 differs in several respects from the other lists. Some practical gifts are included which don't appear elsewhere, for example, 'service' and 'giving' and 'mercy'. These have been designated 'motivational gifts', meaning that each person is naturally disposed to an identifiable approach to the working out of their faith. They define what we **are**, rather than what we **do** necessarily. This is what each person instinctively **wants** to do, rather than feeling that they should.

So for a 'server' it comes naturally to serve. It is his first response to a problem. Christ's servant nature is manifest in his attitudes and actions, but without the strain of effort. He finds God at work in the mundane.

Of course, we will have a mixture of gifts, but one or two will be dominant. This is not the place to look at this aspect exhaustively, only to note that we all have different gifts and these should be recognised and valued, as Paul exhorts us in Romans 12. These descriptions include a positive and negative side to personality, and are what we call our 'nature', what we're born with. 'Nurture' is the influence of our environment and up-bringing: both the fostering of our qualities and the damage inflicted on our personalities by other people and our experiences. God's healing is the process whereby we learn to value our unique personalities, overcome our misgivings about ourselves, address the negative elements and become fully human in relation to Him.

Martha and Mary: service and mercy

"Martha, Martha! You are so worried and troubled over so many things." (Luke 10:41)

Martha has had a bad press over the years, the inference being that she is less spiritual than her sister Mary *"who sat down at the feet of the Lord and listened to His teaching." (Luke 10:39).* Jesus is not criticizing her service. He speaks compassionately. He knows her heart. He is simply making an observation. True, her fussing over details and her complaining demonstrates a negative attitude which needs healing, but her desire to show her love to Jesus in practical ways is commendable.

The home, at Bethany, is described as Martha's. She was the hostess. It is clear that her innate motivational gift was 'serving' - finding joy in the mundane. She would have a pragmatic approach to situations. There is a bit of 'ruling' thrown in as she appears dominant and driving. She likes to believe what she can see and handle, rather than what is hidden and intuitive. The person with this gift likes to see things done properly, and wants to involve other people in the work, under her direction, of course!

We can imagine her dismay when the famous teacher and His entourage invaded her home! There would have been plenty of work to do, and she would have wanted to make the meal really special. Maybe she wanted to impress Him. Perhaps she thought that she could win His love by her good actions.

The relationship with her sister, with whom she lived as an adult, brought pressure upon her: close family relationships often bring out the worst in us! Martha's main fault was self-sufficiency; she would be used to being in control. Like many of us who clutter our lives with unnecessary burdens, she could not understand her sister who was mesmerized by Jesus, and just not aware of Martha's perception of hospitality. She wanted Mary to be like her!

Jesus does not want to change her desire to serve. He simply wants her to be relaxed about it, take a simpler approach. If she had sat at His feet she might have learned peace. He does teach her and bring her to healing in the second incident recorded about Mary and Martha.

"Mary has chosen the better part." (Luke 10: 42 N.R.S.V)
Mary, it appears, has gone to the 'top of the class'. She is single-minded, she wants to learn as much from Jesus as she can. We could describe her motivational gift as dominantly "mercy". Her character is dreamy, a deep thinker, sensitive and impractical. She would have deep feelings of her own and empathy with others. She would identify with those who weep, laugh with those that laugh. We should add an element of the "prophetic", hungry to hear from God, regardless of the cost, focussed on

worship and prayer, having insight into spiritual things. She has chosen the treasures that will last, and Jesus commends her.

This does not mean that she was without faults. No doubt Martha had reason to be exasperated with her. Maybe she frequently had to bring Mary down to earth. We see later that Mary is emotional. She experiences extreme mood swings, is easily hurt and requires protection.

"If You had been here, Lord, my brother would not have died." (John 11:21)
Martha, not Mary, is the speaker. Their brother, Lazarus, Jesus' dear friend has died. Jesus knew that Lazarus was seriously ill but He had delayed four days before he went to Bethany. The sisters heard that Jesus had arrived. Martha rushed out to meet him, but Mary stayed in the house. She was weeping accompanied by an official group of women mourners, which was the tradition when somebody died. It would have been a mournful, hopeless sound, exacerbating the despair of death.

From our previous experience of the character of the two sisters, we would expect Mary to be the one who turned to Jesus for comfort. Instead we find Martha expressing her hope. She has learned to trust in the dark. She goes on to say: "*I know that even now God will give You whatever You ask Him for.*" (*John 11: 21*)

The situation is out of Martha's control. You can't argue with death, so she is throwing herself on Jesus' mercy. It is evident that Martha has taken Jesus' previous advice.

She has listened to His teaching, seen Him perform miracles, and is now expressing her dependency and faith in Him. Jesus claims that anyone who believes in Him will never die. Martha probably doesn't understand the full implication of this, but she declares her conviction that He is the Messiah, the Son of God. She runs with renewed hope to get her sister. Gone now is the peremptory demanding approach. She speaks *"privately"* *(John 11:25)*, tactfully, gently, quietly - just letting her sister know that Jesus is here. Mary is still crying when she sees Jesus and then she says the same thing as Martha did at the outset. *"Lord, if You had been here my brother would not have died!" (John 11: 32)*

But she stops there and so it is a cry of despair - as evidenced in her continued weeping and that of the other wailing women. Jesus is deeply moved, not with grief for He already knows what God intends to come out of this situation: *"This illness will not be the death of Lazarus." (John 11: 4)*. Jesus' tears are because of their unbelief. Mary has spent much time with Him, but at this test of her faith, she gives in to her emotions.

Jesus gives the order to take the stone away from Lazarus' tomb, and the ever practical Martha points out that after four days the body will be rather smelly! But Jesus ignores her, and raised Lazarus from the dead with a word of command: *"Lazarus, come out!" (John11: 43.)*

This seems to be a traumatic process of healing. But we find that the sisters' basic personality has not changed. Martha is still a server: Mary still a mystic. The drama of abject despair turning to amazed joy in the event they have witnessed, has moderated the negative aspects of their characters. They too have experienced resurrection - in their personalities.

When we meet them again at Bethany, a few days later, Jesus again comes to dinner. *(John 12).* Lazarus is there. It must have been an extraordinary experience, almost surreal, but in revisiting the same scenario, with this added extra of having a man who had been dead sitting now at the table, Jesus provides evidence of the inner healing of the two sisters. They have opportunity to exercise their gifts and devotion to Jesus in new-found freedom.

It is stated that **they** made Him supper, although Martha served. Mary had learned to help, and Martha had allowed her to do so. There is no evidence of her former tension in the hostess role. Then Mary makes a very extravagant gesture of her devotion and gratitude to Jesus. She anoints Jesus' feet with a generous amount of very expensive perfume and wipes them with her hair, which meant she was kneeling before Him. The scent filled the whole house. Mary is exploring the full extent of her depths of feeling. She is oblivious of all else in her worship.

This was a typically impractical act on Mary's part, but the criticism does not come from her sister, but from Judas Iscariot, who has ulterior motives. But Mary still needs the protective words of Jesus' commendation. She is still sensitive and vulnerable. He notes that the anointing is prophetic of His death and burial. Mary has again acted from the heart and spiritual motivations rather than from identified knowledge.

Jesus knows and understands us. All He wants is for us to be ourselves, but at the same time relaxed in His presence.

Notes: Ministry

When taking part in prayer ministry:
1.   Listen for those people who undervalue themselves or their service to God. Help them to see the value God puts on them, and that His gifts are not always spectacular.
2.   Listen for the clues that the person is comparing themselves unfavourably with others.
3.   Give opportunity, if you can, for the person to exercise their unique gifts.
4.   Pray for the anointing of the Holy Spirit, and expect God to confirm their gift, and make them ready to receive other gifts.

Chapter 4
Rebirth not just Reform

"When my bones were being formed, carefully put together in my mother's womb, when I was growing there in secret, you knew I was there - You saw me before I was born." (Psalm 139:15)

"I feel as if I have been remade from my mother's womb." The young woman had received ministry, and for about fifteen minutes had been 'resting in the Lord'. A word of knowledge had informed the ministers that she had been traumatised before birth. *"Do not be surprised if I tell you that you must all be born again." (John 3:7.)*

Nicodemus is confused by Jesus' insisting that we need to start life all over again. *"How can a grown man be born again? He certainly cannot enter his mother's womb and be born a second time!" (John 3: 4).* But Jesus insists that our salvation is not just a matter of tweaking the edges of our personality here and there. God created each of us for a unique purpose. He wants us to realise that purpose and to become the person He intended us to be. When Jesus was born, he had a human mother, but God was His Father. His human life then was all God intended Him to be, a model of perfect humanity. We had no such natural inheritance, because we were born as fallen human beings. Our spiritual life was deadened to awareness of God and this has caused damage within us. Jesus died that we might be restored into that relationship with God as our Father.

In order to make that effective, we have to start all over again. This is what inner healing is about. The Holy Spirit does nothing less than taking the genetic material and enabling it to grow through all the stages, unravel the damage, until the person is wholly remade. This of course, is never completed in our lifetimes, mostly because we are largely unaware of the scope of the need - and there is a lot of work to do! That does not daunt the Holy Spirit, though. From the moment we are born of the Spirit, He starts this work in us.

Note that we **are** born; it is a passive experience, just as physical birth is. We may cooperate with the birth process, but we can hardly resist it. For this reason we cannot be sure when the Holy Spirit in any one case begins to work in us. When we find out we are born, we sense this new way of being. In physical birth, it is chilly compared to the warmth of the womb; we take our first breath and make our first sound - a yell! There may be a sense of loss. We are out of the security of being constantly nourished and we become hungry and, at times, uncomfortable and need attention.

Similarly in rebirth, we will begin to notice a change in our way of being, and in our perception of need. Our spirits have come alive and need feeding. We have become aware of God and His legitimate demands upon us; our need to change the corruption of the beauty that He had created in our lives. One cogent definition of sin is that it is a spoiling of God's creation. So we respond, we confess that sin, ask forgiveness, and ask God to begin to effect that change. This is the prayer He is waiting for -

so that He can joyfully answer it, and when we give our full cooperation, He can put His plans for us into operation.

Biblical case study
A man blind from birth: recreated

"One thing I do know: I was blind, and now I see."
(John 9:25)

It was a simple statement of fact, and unarguable. This man had been blind from birth. Anyone who knew him knew that this was true. He had known no other life; the world had been dark and colourless to him. He had been a beggar, dependent on others for his livelihood. He would only be able to find his way about by use of his other senses.

Jesus' disciples had asked Him a theological question: *"Teacher, whose sin caused him to be born blind? Was it his own or his parents' sin?"* (*John 9:2.*) Jesus had brushed the question aside. It is irrelevant, since all sickness and disability is the result of the fall of man. When sin came into the world it was accompanied by all manner of destructive elements. In the Greek there is no punctuation, so Jesus replied: *"But that the works of God may be made manifest in him I must work the works of Him that sent me God while it is day." (John 9: 3, 4a A.V.)*

He had been referring to Himself previously: *"I am the Light of the world." (John 8:12.)* The man who had been

born blind demonstrates the darkness which is in every person when Jesus is not present. The work of God is to reverse the fall and to restore mankind to wholeness. John records Jesus' commentary on this event. His miracles were done out of compassion for those who suffer, but they also have meaning beyond the immediate.

"I came into this world to judge, so that the blind should see and those who see should become blind."
(John 9: 39).

The blind man, after he had obeyed Jesus' command to go and wash in the pool of Siloam, clearly experienced a "rebirth"; his life from the womb was transformed in every way. Some of his friends did not recognise him. It wasn't just that he could see. His whole outlook had changed. He was no longer just a beggar and to be pitied. He was the talk of the town!

He is naturally bewildered by the sudden turn of events, but he is confident enough to be cheeky even to the religious leaders who challenge him. His understanding of who Jesus is develops slowly but is provoked by their unbelief, and spiritual blindness. At first he just sticks to the basic facts. He doesn't know much so he testifies to what he does know, and gradually this leads him to recognise the identity of the Person who healed him. Then, when asked, he gives the opinion that Jesus is a prophet. He is exasperated when they challenge him a third time; he protests that he has already told them. He asks them if they too want to follow Jesus!

The religious leaders are incensed and say that they do not know where Jesus has come from. It was enough for the man who had been blind to experience the miracle to know that Jesus had come from God. The religious leaders are not happy with his answer, and ban him from the synagogue. It is unlikely that the man was very much upset by this. After all, he could now see!

Finally, he encounters Jesus again, and Jesus asks him if he believes in the Son of Man, that is the Anointed One of God - the Messiah. The man asks Jesus to tell him who that is. Jesus reveals Himself to him, and the man immediately worships Him. He has been utterly transformed, made to see physically, and in his mind and in his spirit.

Notes: Ministry

When taking part in prayer ministry:

1. It is not necessary always for a person to remember a trauma for it to be healed. A word of knowledge may reveal an incident that happened even before birth, or a suppressed memory.
2. When you pray for the person, in such a case, it is better just to let the Holy Spirit do His work of rebirth.
3. Dreams are a good indicator of the nature of suppressed memories.
   In sleep the conscious mind is switched off and the sub-conscious mind has freedom to

express itself. If dreams are mentioned, concentrate on the emotions that have been aroused, more than the symbolism.

4. Take care! Memories are suppressed for a reason - usually because the person is not ready to face them. The fact that they have surfaced, however, in the presence of the Holy Spirit, may well mean that He wants to heal them. Gentle reassurance that God does everything in love is the best approach.

5. Make sure that if there has been a dramatic change in the life of the person that they are aware that they need to take time for adjustment. They may well sleep a lot after ministry. Often in sleep God does a deep healing work.

Chapter 5
Religion or Reality?

"Jesus answered: 'If you were blind then you would not be guilty; but since you claim that you can see, this means you are still guilty'". (John 9:41)

"You need to be careful. You don't want to raise people's expectations too much or they may be disappointed." Common sense rules O.K! We have not experienced the power of God, so we must stick with what we know. We don't want people hurt or confused. The final comment by Jesus on the incident of the healing of the man who had been born blind, was that the religious leaders could not see what was right under their noses - the power of God made manifest. One of the greatest barriers to a relationship with the living God is religion.

"When we talk of religious activities this is a far different concept than the dreary old stone buildings in which worship was made to an omnipotent "God" who ruled by fear." This is a recent quote about the Christian church in Britain from an advertisement by a leader of a New Age pagan movement. What an indictment! Fear of extremism, of offending our cultural mores, upsetting our compromising middle-class values, of stepping out in risky faith has caused a large part of the church in Western countries to water down the Gospel. We have reduced our faith to mental assent to rituals and rules. We have peddled an image of a joyless, powerless, positively boring God. We are as blind as the Pharisees, Sadducees and other Jewish religious leaders of Jesus day. How we need to repent, believe God's Word, and act on it! Religion has crushed our spiritual understanding and limited the horizons of our lives, created resistance to the Holy Spirit's influence. But where He can, Jesus sets about healing those wounds in individuals.

Biblical case study
Jairus: *"Talitha koum - arise!"* (*Mark 5:41 A.V.*)

This is not so much the story of the Jairus' daughter as of Jairus himself and his growth in faith. Jairus was the ruler of the synagogue, the administrative head and responsible for the good management of the synagogue. He oversaw the services there, allocating the duties and making sure that everything was done in good order. He would be one of the most important and respected men in the community.

As a member of the orthodox religious elite, he would have heard the critics of Jesus who rejected Him as the Messiah, vilified Him as a dangerous heretic, distorted and despised everything He did, explained away His miracles, and emphasized His breaking of the Sabbath and other rules of Judaism. He would have been prejudiced against Him, and would know that approaching Him with anything but suspicion would lose him his friends and associates and his reputation in society.

All that was put aside when his beloved daughter fell gravely ill. He was desperate: she was dying. He had broken through the large crowd surrounding Jesus; he had to persist against the wall of people. He had to expose his need. He humbled himself by falling at Jesus' feet and pleading with Him to heal his daughter. His religious pride and his dignity were in tatters. He expresses a small measure of faith in that he expected his daughter to get well if Jesus laid hands on her, but, at this stage, he may not have recognised who Jesus was. The testimonies of healings that he had heard, even from critical lips, made him ready to try this last resort to save his daughter.

Even then, as Jesus started out with Jairus, there was an interruption, which distracted Jesus, and He allowed it to do so. He stopped to minister to the woman who had an issue of blood. He could have ignored her, but chose not to. This was not just for her sake, although that was paramount, but also for Jairus' sake. He needed to know that Jesus not only had the power to heal, but also to restore a dead person to life, which would totally transform Jairus' preconceived notions. Jesus was not just another itinerant preacher with some mystical powers, but the One who has the power over death, and Jairus knew well the scriptures which foretold the characteristics of the longed-for Messiah.

So now Jesus, who knew His own power in the Holy Spirit, as He did later with Lazarus, delays long enough for the child to die. Jairus is further humiliated by the suspiciously quick action of members of his household who rush to tell him not to bother the Teacher any more, not to waste His time, because the little girl has died. It is likely that they had not been in favour of his petition to Jesus in the first place. The hopelessness of the situation is fed by this news, but Jesus counters it with a direct word to Jairus: *"Don't be afraid, only believe." (Mark 5: 36b).*

The word for fear used here and mostly elsewhere in the New Testament had the meaning of flight caused by terror and dread. This reflects Jesus appreciation of Jairus' reaction of shock. Jesus is telling him not to give up at this point: faith overcomes fear. It was enough for Jairus to follow Jesus along with the three most trusted of His disciples to Jairus' house.

Jesus was not playing a cruel game with Jairus. He had a greater object in mind. Jairus has to go through this process in order to receive healing himself. So often Jesus identifies that which is our most precious thing. He allows us to suffer loss in order to expose our greatest fears and our wrong concepts about the goodness of God. Jairus, the respected, wealthy man, once in authority and in control of his life, is now helpless in the face of tragedy.

As they approach the house, the prospect of the triumph of faith is made dimmer by the tumult of grief. The professional mourners redouble their efforts. The little girl was twelve years old - in Jewish culture a virgin on the verge of womanhood. It was all the more tragic. Worse still, her father had been absent on a fool's errand, when she had died. Jairus' fear is now compounded by guilt. His problem has reached rock-bottom. It is gross. Jesus' words of reassurance are mocked by the mourners, and the sounds of their mirthless ridicule are echoing in their ears as Jesus takes the child's parents and the disciples into the room where she is lying.

Jairus obeys in bewilderment. He has no resistance left. Jesus takes calm, serene control. He will not allow anyone into the room that will not co-operate with Him. He is not there to counsel or console the bereaved, but to revitalise the situation. He takes hold of her by the hand. The implication is that He gets possession of her, winning her back to His sphere of existence. In Aramaic, her mother tongue, *"Talitha koum"* (Mark 5:41), He speaks straight into her spirit with simplicity and quiet authority, and tells her to get up. She immediately does so. As proof that she is alive and not a ghost, He suggests they feed her. Maybe too Jesus wants to bring them back down to earth after this revelation of His power. They are not dreaming; this is real and happening now. The direct translation of the Greek text emphasizes their amazement at this turn of events: *"They were astonished with a great astonishment." (Mark 5: 42 A.V).*

The word for astonishment is the root word for ecstasy, a standing out, being taken out of oneself, a trance. It implies that they are overcome, perhaps numbed, speechless and immobilized. Temporarily they too have been brought to the point of death – the death of their values and attitudes to life. Now they are experiencing a glorious resurrection into the reality of God. He is no longer just a distant, rather stern judge, a figure in a rather stale book of rituals and obligations. He is alive and cares about our needs and takes redemptive action. Their whole focus has changed, not by persuasion, but by demonstration.

The Word spoken in the Holy Spirit speaks not just to the mind but to the spirits of men and women recreating their whole beings. The gentle caress of the words *"Talitha koum"* would reverberate in their minds, as it had evidently in the mind of the writer of the Gospel, bringing constant encouragement and hope for years to come.

Notes: Ministry

When taking part in prayer ministry:

1. Listen for anything in their story which binds them to religious rules or rituals. These are strong barriers to a living relationship with Jesus.
2. Similarly listen for legalistic attitudes. These misdirect people from the unconditional grace of God.
3. Express God's grace, that salvation and healing is not dependent on our good works or any special rituals.
4. In the midst of their tragic story, minister the healing power of Jesus. Let Him surprise and delight them.

Chapter 6
Seeds and Weeds

"The owner's servants came to him and said: 'Sir, didn't you sow good seed in your field? Where then did the weeds come from?!'
'An enemy did this,' he replied." (Matthew 13: 27, 28. N.I.V.)

I don't have the first idea about gardening. I can remember the first time I decided to turn a small bit of rough ground outside our mobile home into a garden. I dug and forked and sweated, turning over the turfs and plants, and levelling the ground.

I looked out of the window with pride onto to this gleaming, chocolate brown earth, rubbed my sore back, then turned my attention to my very small children. I had a busy week and it rained continuously so I didn't get the chance to get out and do any planting in my new garden. When I looked out of the window at the end of that week I was horrified to see that the brown was rapidly turning green again. The very weeds I had so industriously buried, but not pulled up, were sprouting up all over the place!

"I the Lord your God am a jealous God, visiting the iniquity of the fathers on the children, on the third and the fourth generation of those who hate me." (Exodus 20:5. N.A.S.B.)
One of the first principles of the process of inner healing is to recognise that most of us are more sinned against

than sinning. The enemy wreaks havoc and injury in our lives by using traumatic events to create lasting damage. Sin, as we call it, is usually a reaction to the way we have been treated ourselves. We are still morally responsible to prevent or correct that reaction but often it is quite involuntary and irrational and we ourselves don't even understand why we behave in such a way.

The image of a garden is helpful. As small children, babies, or even before we are born, we are virgin soil, innocent, not morally responsible but vulnerable to every influence upon our lives. We cannot defend ourselves from any assault, and it is then that the weeds of our later sins are sown. Unfortunately, as we have seen, it is those who are closest to us: our parents, our siblings and other close relatives who are, often quite inadvertently and unknowingly, responsible for sowing these seeds.

They, themselves are "sinners", they too had seeds sown in their lives which make them react. These seeds have their own characteristics. The plant grows and develops because of the genetic structure of its "parent" seed. So if we are, for example victimised in childhood by verbal abuse, we grow up overly sensitive to any perceived criticism, and maybe react with irrational anger or acute self-consciousness.

Even the best parents make mistakes. How often have we said that really we ought to have two separate broods of children: the first brood is the draft copy? We make our mistakes, learn from them, and, in the wisdom of age, bring up a second brood with perfected parenting skills. We wish! And poor first brood!

As children and adults, we want so much to gain the approval of our parents, right until the day they die. My own mother, I know, loved me dearly, but unfortunately, she recognised my noisy, lively assertive nature, a reflection of her own, encouraged me to do my little "party pieces" and make people laugh. Then, very soon afterwards, she would scold me for "showing off". The mixed messages confused my young developing mind and I carried the confusion into adult life, both proud of my strong presence in social situations - the ability to be the "life and soul of the party" – but also embarrassed by the attention, reactions, and often jealousy it incurred.

More seriously it intruded into my concept of ministry, until it was addressed and healed. God wants to use our personalities, our consecrated natural as well as spiritual gifts and our sense of humour. Once we recognise that he loves what He made, we can become ourselves, but sometimes we need the assistance and insight of others in the process of relearning and self-appraisal.

Sometimes these traumas are sourced in a trauma in the womb, as we saw in Chapter 4 and the study in the life of the man born blind. It has been proved by experiment that babies can see, hear, taste, smell and feel well before they are born. They react to loud noises. Those whose mothers were pregnant during the blitz of the Second World War are often sensitive to sudden loud noises, and react with irrational fear. They have picked up their mother's emotions without knowing what they were.

My own mother was carrying me during the war. She already had two little boys under five years old. She was living in very difficult circumstances, in the wilds of Yorkshire. She wanted to be near my father who had been posted to an air-field nearby. She found herself in an isolated, small, draughty cottage, heated by a wood-burning stove, having to draw water from a well, and feeding herself and my brothers on war-time rations.

Then she discovered that she was pregnant with me. I heard her relate this story, with bitterness, repeatedly very late into her long life. One day the penny dropped, and I made the connections. This bitterness and sense of insecurity sowed seeds into my life. She cherished and cared for me when I was finally born in a poorly resourced nursing home. She saved my life three times in my early years by common-sense and determined intervention.

The third time was when I, suddenly, at the tender age of two and a-half years, developed acute arthritis in my right leg, accompanied by an extremely high, life-threatening temperature and the side effect of rheumatic fever, which should create a weakness in the valves of the heart. She ignored the advice of the local GP, who had sent her home with a bottle of aspirins overnight. She marched into the local hospital with me in her arms, pushing past the receptionists and other waiting patients and waited until someone came out of the consultant's office. There she thrust open the door and plonked me down in front of the astonished doctor. He took one look at the blackened, grossly swollen ankle and leg and the clearly feverish child and admitted me into emergency care where my life was saved by the prompt use of a drug new to the civilian population - penicillin.

I recovered, but the disease left me with a legacy of chronic arthritis, settled in my joints which recurred throughout my life whenever I got really wet or cold. I was told that I should beware of ever breaking a bone, and that I would be crippled with the disease in old age. I have no legacy of heart disease because my mother's intervention was timely. But the other warnings remained as a curse upon my life until about three years ago when I saw the connection between bitterness and arthritis, and was healed.

There are, of course, those who are deliberately cruel and wicked to satisfy their own lusts. The victims of child abuse carry these scars of guilt, shame and pain all their lives. Medical professionals recognise this, and, of course, we as active co-workers with the Lord can honour and cooperate with these practitioners. But even counselling and radical prolonged psychotherapy often does not heal these wounds.

But Jesus does! He can reach down, reveal the root cause, identify the seed which was sown, and the event which allowed it to flourish, even when we can't remember it ourselves. Sometimes the trauma seems trivial and exaggerated to the adult mind, but to the mind of a child it takes on the proportion of an earthquake in their safe, self-centred world where everything they imagine should be designed to serve their needs and emotional stability.

Many times I have heard people who have been through a tedious counselling process, expressing that they really don't want to tell their life stories all over again. The Holy Spirit can reveal the nature and timing of the original seed to the listening Christian, by a word of knowledge, and the weed is pulled out by its roots, and the process of healing begins.

I was taught, as I say, by the Holy Spirit. I sometimes received a word of knowledge, not always labelling it as such but simply testing it out, tentatively at first. I remember well one of the first times I realised what the Holy Spirit was doing. I was running a summer camp for children at the school where I taught Religious Education. One of the junior group leaders came to me in perplexity about one of the young girls in her charge. This girl was about eleven years old, but behaved more like a six year old. She exuded unhappiness, apparently could not enjoy the fun activities of camp life and was very insecure, perhaps because she was away from her home and family for the first time.

But the leader explained that she was constantly in a state of panic complaining that "someone had stolen her money or possessions", and always a subsequent search of the area around her bunk bed in the dormitory or her baggage revealed that she had hidden the item herself but had forgotten she had done so. At the table she would sit with both arms circling her plate, her head down, but every so often stealing glances at those sitting next to her, and eating awkwardly in this position.

I took the child aside and chatted until she opened up a bit about her life. She came from a large and rather poor family. As she talked, I kept getting an image of a very small wooden toy train painted bright blue, and the words "five years." In the end this image so plagued me that I asked gently: "Have you ever had or seen a little blue wooden toy train?" Her reaction was immediate and dramatic. She spat out viciously: "Yes, I had one for Christmas when I was five - and my brother stole it and broke it up - and I hate him!"

It does not take a Masters degree in Psychology to work out the connection! The seed was identified and rooted out. We prayed for healing and the child's behaviour and general demeanour began to change from that moment. The way the Holy Spirit taught me to pray and minister in many similar situations will be discussed later in this book.

Sometimes the shaping of our lives as we give ourselves to God can in itself address the weeds and reverse the effect of the enemy's work, without the intervention of direct ministry. We shall see this as we study the biblical case studies. For the moment let it be known:
"But the godly shall flourish like palm trees, and grow tall as the cedars of Lebanon. For they are transplanted into

God's own garden, and are under His personal care."
(Psalm 92:12, 13. L.B.)

Biblical case study
Joseph's garden: a life weeded and cultivated through experience
Genesis Chapter 37ff

If the life of Joseph, the son of Jacob and Rachel, can be seen as a garden of God, he was planted with precious spiritual seeds, but also the enemy sowed his seeds of deceit. His father Jacob had already sired ten sons, but Joseph was Rachel's first-born. As we have seen in Chapter 2, the beautiful Rachel was Jacob's first love, but Jacob was tricked into marrying first her older sister, Leah, who was less attractive. Rachel seemed to be barren - a source of great shame to a Jewish mother. Her older sister, Leah, was deemed to be favoured by God, because she was the mother of five of Jacob's twelve children. After Jacob also took as wives the sisters' two slave-girls, as was the custom of the day, five more sons were born to him. Finally Rachael gave birth to Joseph, but she chose that name because it meant "May I have another", and subsequently produced the youngest son, Benjamin.

So, Joseph's entry into the world was accompanied by mixed messages: he was a favourite son of his father, but not enough for his mother. Her attitude would have sowed the seeds of his underlying insecurity which often results in a tendency to be over-assertive, cocky and critical of others in order to boost his own image. His father compounded this by demonstrating his favour to Joseph by giving him privileges, listening to his 'cliping' about his brothers' behaviour, and by giving him a specially ornamented tunic. By the time he was seventeen years he was quite frankly a spoiled brat—and his brothers hated him.

It seems though that Joseph was also favoured by God. He had dreams which foretold, quite accurately, his future supremacy over his father and brothers. But he didn't have the sense to keep this information to himself. So the brat also became a boaster which reduced his "street cred." with his brothers even more—though not with his father who pondered it and no doubt thought that his precious son would finally surface as the top dog.

All this was bound to end in tears. His brothers seized him out in the field, sold him to slave traders, and reported his 'death' to his Jacob, who promptly transferred his inordinate affection on Rachel's and his younger son, Benjamin. God clearly had plans for Joseph. But first he had to get the weeds out of the garden of his life.

It appears that Joseph was sorely tried by God. First he was sold into slavery in Egypt, then falsely accused of rape and finally imprisoned without trial. In each of these humiliating situations, however, the Joseph's true mettle shone out. He always surfaced as a leader of men. His masters recognised his hard work, his willingness to undertake even the most menial tasks and his evident integrity. Most of all Joseph retained his trust in the God who had spoken to his spirit in dreams as a child.

Joseph's character was honed by his experiences and the seeds of pride rooted out. Pharaoh eventually was introduced to him. It was again through a dream - Pharaoh's own - which Joseph accurately interpreted for him and Joseph's worth was recognised. He indeed became a ruler, second only to Pharaoh, and the one who organized the provisions for the seven-year famine which affected Egypt and all the countries round about. This was what he himself had predicted.

God's mercy in his dealings with his chosen vessel became evident because then his childhood dream was fulfilled. His brothers came down to Egypt seeking food during the famine in Canaan. Not recognizing their brother in his exalted role, they bowed low, grovelling to obtain his favour and a ration of food for their starving family.

But the story does not end there: Joseph's garden was weeded, but the plant needed to be moved into a wider location so that the seed can be recognised as originating in the love of God. We will return later to this story, in Chapter 7, to witness the completion of his inner healing.

Notes: Ministry

When taking part in prayer ministry:

1. In listening to the person's story, don't get tangled up in detail - especially if they have been a long-term patient of psychiatric or psychological professionals. Ask God to highlight the significant factors.
2. In your questions, mirror those factors back to the person.
3. Again, look for repeated patterns of behaviour.
4. Be careful not to discount what might appear to be a trivial event or hurt. Remember people have different levels of coping and what maybe of paramount importance to them means very little to someone else. It is not what we experience, but how we cope with it that counts.
5. Recognise where the enemy has sown lies and curses into a person's life, causing them to they live in fear.
Refute these and apply truth. Be bold to relate words of knowledge, scriptures, pictures etc. which may indicate the "seed" of the person's problem. Stay with that. It may be enough for the time being to identify and deal with that. Their problems may then begin to wither as the plant is uprooted.

Chapter 7:
Forgiving but Remembering

In the film, "The Mission", the hero is a Roman Catholic missionary priest, who before his conversion to Christ had been a soldier and was responsible for the deaths of many enemies. He is deeply remorseful and he imposes upon himself a form of penance. He is strong and agile but he elects to get a bag full of heavy metal objects up a very steep cliff beside a waterfall. It is treacherously slippery and difficult enough even for someone unladen. He drops the net or slips back frequently, but he struggles on, sweating profusely, and with his back scoured by the rope. He eventually arrives at the top and drops to the ground totally exhausted. He then has to negotiate thick forest, full of poisonous insects, marauding beasts and peopled by murderous and stealthy Indians who resent his presence. They pick off his men with poison-tipped arrows.

I was left feeling that the poor man had enough to contend with in the environment without going through such a self-imposed ordeal. Forgiveness is of primary importance in the process of inner healing. Unforgiveness is a self-imposed burden which has little effect on the one who needs forgiveness, and is much more likely to destroy the person carrying it.

Unforgiveness produces morbid states of mind: fear, resentment, and defeat -- attitudes which spill over and infect all our relationships. Adults who have been abused as children often carry the burden of guilt and desire for revenge for many years, whilst the perpetrators may live their lives carefree. Often such offenders excuse their behaviour by a perverted attitude. They do not take guilt on board. Parents who have lost children to predators will wrestle with bitter grief until the abductor is found and brought to justice. They speak of "closure" at this point but yell abuse at the one convicted, and are clearly under tremendous strain.

Bitterness and unforgiveness is proven to be the root cause of many mental and physical complaints. The stress builds up in the body and causes the secretion of acids and the result can be stomach ulcers, cancer or severe arthritis. It is well-known that approximately two years after a divorce settlement, one of the parties often experiences stomach complaints - it happened to me!

"Forgive them, Father! They don't know what they are doing." (Luke 23:34.) *"As far as the east is from the west, so far does He remove our sins from us." (Psalm 103:12)* The first step in unravelling unforgiveness is the person's recognition of it, followed by confession of distorted attitudes and spoiled relationships. Encourage the person to be very specific. This recognition of our own fault is hard when we have been deeply hurt, and many say that they cannot forgive. We need to recognise that our wills need assistance at these times. *"For God is at work within you, helping you to want to obey Him, and then helping you to do what He wants." (Philippians 2:13 L.B.)*

God redeemed our wills at Gethsemane, when Jesus chose to take the cup of suffering for us, and go to the cross. Corrie Ten Boom, a Dutch Christian imprisoned in a concentration camp during World War Two, recorded an incident where feelings certainly were not enough. Her sister had suffered greatly at the hands of a German guard who acted as an orderly in the camp hospital. Corrie remembered him well as a cruel captor who neglected and abused her sister who eventually died. Many years later Corrie was a travelling evangelist who spoke of the love of God even in a concentration camp. She had been speaking on the need for forgiveness even of our worst enemies.

After the meeting a tired looking old man approached her. When he introduced himself, she recognised him as that guard and her instinct was to turn away from him in disgust. He begged her forgiveness, and Corrie cried out to God. She records that she could not raise her eyes or her hand to meet that man halfway. She was facing the very challenge she had just proclaimed herself!

As the guard pleaded, Corrie collected herself and asked God to give her the will to take him by the hand and pronounce the words he longed to hear. She said as soon as she prayed that prayer, it was as if an unseen hand lifted hers into his. She found herself clasping his hand in hers, and amidst floods of tears on both sides, she said simply "I forgive you", and the pain of years drained away.

Forgiveness, indeed, is a powerful agent; it carries a spiritual force which can travel across time and distance. Two sisters in America, we'll call them Annie and May, had quarrelled in their late teens. They swore never to speak again. They both moved away and lost contact for over forty years. Annie, now in her early seventies, became a Christian and felt convicted to seek reconciliation with her sister, but she had no idea where she was. Her counsellor suggested that she bring May's face to mind, picturing their last quarrel , and in that moment declare out loud her forgiveness and her need for forgiveness.

Only a few weeks later, May called her. She had been moved to find Annie and be reconciled, and had trawled all the means of tracking her down that were possible, and had succeeded. There was a joyful and tearful reunion.

Unforgiveness is like a boil, it needs to be lanced, and all the poison released.
I remember the first time I was able to explain to an American Pastor the circumstances of my unhappy marriage. He stopped me in mid-sentence and told me that I shouldn't excuse the perpetrator, or minimize the pain, but I should "tell it like it is". He was right - the truth needs to be faced.

One way of leading a hurting person to forgiveness, is to ask them to recall the person who hurt them, and a situation where that person inflicted pain upon them. Look into their face, and pronounce, out loud, if possible, their forgiveness. This can be followed by blessing the person who hurt them. This ensures that if we have been honest about their actions, we are not left with mere gossip which is destructive. Words, especially those spoken by Christians, are powerful spiritual tools. If we bless someone we can counteract a curse or negative criticism.

Sometimes the person who needs to be forgiven is our self. Dave (not his real name), was now a Christian, but he had been a member of a city gang who, under the influence of drink or drugs, inflicted severe injury , sometimes resulting in the death of members of rival gangs. He was full of guilt and blamed himself for a knife fight from which his victim never recovered. We showed him how Jesus had been in that traumatic situation, grieving for Dave himself, as well as the dying victim. As we declared that Jesus had gone to the cross to obtain Dave's forgiveness, so that Dave had no business to carry the guilt. When the penny had dropped, we suggested that he picture his own face as in a mirror, and declare his forgiveness for the man he had been but in Christ no longer was. His relief at the end of this exercise was palpable.

Occasionally we come across someone who blames God for their sufferings. Some think that God is punishing them for something they have done. This lie is to be confronted and refuted. God is good and His love is unconditional. The blood of Jesus shed on the cross covers all sin and sickness.

"Forgive the wrongs we have done <u>as</u> we forgive the wrongs that others have done to us." (*Matthew 6:12*)

There is a tank filled with forgiveness in the roof-space of our souls. God is yearning to release it to us, but it is sealed in the pipes leading from the tank until we turn on a tap. That tap is the act of forgiveness released to someone else. It is not a gooey and mushy feeling which motivates us to reach out emotionally and forgive. It is a robust act of will which recognises the destructive power of continuing resentment, and the creative power of releasing the object of our bitterness.

My husband was mentally ill. Five years of dominance by him, of being knocked into submission verbally and physically, left a legacy in my life which persisted in a number of ways for several years. A large part of my healing from this relationship has been forgiveness. This I exercised from the beginning of the marriage as hurts piled upon hurts, for truly 'he didn't know what he was doing'. He was ill and out of control; he could not help it. I just happened to be the object on which his frustration and delusion could be fastened.

But it left its legacy. I had trouble with relationships particularly with strong male leadership. This made it difficult for me to share ministry with them and specifically take criticism and advice without resentment and fear. When this was revealed to me in one particular situation, I asked the current strong leader to pray with me for my healing, which he did and I felt a measure of release. But I had to address several more in the same way, (much to their bewilderment in some cases!) before I could be sure that the reactions were out of my emotional system or at least were recognised as they emerged and I could pray them through on my own.

The final relief and freedom from his brooding influence came when someone, fairly recently, in the spirit cut off the 'soul ties' with him. The term 'soul tie' is applied to a close relationship, often within the bond of family, especially in a sexual relationship (within marriage or extra-marital) which links us inextricably with the other person. God designed sex to make husband and wife "one flesh", in a godly bond. If the tie is ungodly, it takes the power of the Holy Spirit to sever us and release us. My relationship with my second husband who is a gentle and mild-mannered man, contributed much to the healing of these emotions.

In ministry we often long to get to the heart of the matter immediately, and sometimes we do, as we saw when we were discussing "seeds" in chapter 6. But emotions take a long time to heal, and often we have to allow the process to take its course. In the case of mature Christians who are used to self-examination and aware of the grace of God, they can be educated in addressing the problems themselves as they arise, but most need assistance and maybe a counteracting experience to help them through.

The trauma, the hatred of the perpetrator and the most painful memories can be gloriously healed. We don't, as the saying goes, 'forgive and forget'. We continue to hold the memory (unless our brain cells are destroyed by some injury). We know that our inner healing is complete when we can look back on the events and recall those people and see ourselves in those situations, without pain, as if it were a character in some kind of television soap.

Biblical case study
Joseph: transplanted into open ground, watered, fertilized and thriving

"Other seeds fell among thorns and the thorns choked out the tender blades." (Matthew 13:7 L.B.)

The 'thorns' in our lives are not necessarily our circumstances. We are plants in the garden of the Master Husbandman and He knows what needs trimming or rooting out in our lives. Other people and situations do indeed cause us grief, and inner healing addresses that, but the process is not complete until the thornier parts of our characters are weeded - and again adversity and other people who inhabit our worlds may well become the tools for that gardening.

We have already seen this in the life of Joseph. It looks as if God the Gardener had done some radical landscaping in Joseph's life. The story of his replanting and the care of the growing plant is harrowing, and does not look like mercy at all. But here he is prosperous and successful for we left him last time in the scene where his brothers are prostrating themselves before the second most powerful ruler in Egypt, totally unaware that this is their exiled brother, who they had sold into slavery and their actions are fulfilling his childhood dream.

This is the blossoming evidence of Joseph's healing. The scene which unfolds before him is his "action replay" portrayed in the original dream, but rejected and ridiculed. Now he knows that God's Word is reliable and his destiny was ordained, but he has also learned wisdom along the way. He wants to forgive them, but they need healing too - so, under the guidance of God, he sets out to conduct a series of tests. We would expect him to confront his brothers, exult in his triumph, but he does not, at first, make any move to identify himself to them or make any attempt at reconciliation.

It appears that he does exploit his exalted position by making life uncomfortable for them. He accuses them of spying, and puts them all in jail for three days. After this he appears to apply mercy. He releases them and asks them to bring their youngest brother back from Canaan with them when they return. He, of course, knows the duration of the famine by his more recent interpretation of Pharaoh's dream. However, he asks for one to remain as a hostage, and the second oldest brother Simeon is selected.

The brothers discuss the situation in front of Joseph, who has been speaking to them through an interpreter, and so they don't realise that he understands them. They are beginning to show guilt and remorse for their treatment of Joseph, blaming their present predicament on a just retribution for their former sins. Our emotions do not recognise the passage of time, without healing our inner traumas remain raw. Joseph weeps as they express not repentance but their fears of punishment.

He could have given in to sentiment, but instead he gives secret orders to provide food for their journey home and their money to be returned to them in the neck of their sacks of grain. They and their father are dismayed and fearful at this action, and Jacob vetoes the idea that his son, Benjamin, should ever go with them to Egypt. He is the only remaining son of his precious wife, Rachel. When the brothers again are driven by hunger to realise that they would have to make a further visit to Egypt, Judah, Jacob's fourth son, suggests that he take responsibility for Benjamin's safety.

When originally the brothers had decided to get rid of Joseph, the eldest brother, Reuben had begged them not to kill him, and together they had grabbed him and dropped him into the bottom of a dry well, suggesting that they could leave him to die of exposure, but secretly planning to rescue him later. He had then gone away, only to return too late to stop the brothers selling Joseph to the Ishmaelite traders. It was Judah who suggested this, so now we are beginning to see how circumstances have conspired to begin the work of repentance in this brother.

To their bewilderment when they arrive in Egypt they are given royal hospitality in the palace, especially Benjamin who has preferential treatment. Their protests, on arrival, that their money for the previous grain has been returned to them are brushed aside. Joseph asks after their father, and can hardly contain himself for joy when he sees Benjamin. He retreats to weep. He is keeping his emotions to himself though, and again orders that their money be restored to them as before and that his own silver cup is put into Benjamin's sack. The brothers are pursued on the journey home, the cup is discovered and they are arrested and brought back to Joseph. Benjamin is threatened with slavery for "*stealing the cup*". (*Genesis 44:5*) It seems as if Joseph is taking cruel vengeance on the brothers by creating scenarios to tease their consciences.

The outcome of all this psychological pressure, however, is extraordinary. Judah intervenes to explain the story of Joseph's "death" saying that his father would be heart-broken if he lost Benjamin and he pleads with Joseph to let him take Benjamin's place. Judah's repentance, respect and concern for his ailing father and willingness to make amends for his action are evident.

Joseph can stand it no longer and the stage is set for a full reconciliation with his brothers. He clears the room and speaks directly to them in their own tongue. He expresses his forgiveness by getting them to see God's overview of their actions: "*It was God who sent me here, not you!*" *(Genesis 45:7.L.B.)* He sees the plan of God concerning all of them revealed, and his love for God overrides any resentment.

Again we see the Word of God reshaping the actions and words of the trauma, giving His perspective, renewing His grace. The brothers are at first stunned, but the scene that follows overflows with joy and restoration as each one falls into Joseph's welcoming arms. *"And He* (i.e. God the Gardener) *prunes those branches which bear fruit for even larger crops."* (John 15:2a. L.B.)

Notes: Ministry

When taking part in prayer ministry:

1. Emphasise that forgiveness of the perpetrators of damage is essential to a person's inner healing.
2. As the person tells their story of hurt or betrayal, make sure they express the truth.
3. Note when they cannot forgive themselves. Encourage them to accept themselves as they are because God does.
4. Be alert to physical illnesses which may well be rooted in unforgiveness.
5. Lead them, when they are ready, to an act of forgiveness and blessing for the person who hurt them, speaking it out loud if necessary, explaining it is a matter of will, not feeling. (If the person isn't ready, this will have to wait to a later date).
6. Address the most painful, but not necessarily all the incidents. Once the process has started these will naturally fade.
7. Take care if they propose to approach the perpetrator, even expressing forgiveness, as this may do more harm than good. It can only be effective in reconciliation if the Holy Spirit clearly indicates the timing and manner of such an

encounter. If they see such action as essential (as in the case of a close relationship, such as marriage), counsel them to be gentle, tactful and non-confrontational and to introduce the subject by confessing their own faults, especially their lack of forgiveness.

8.   If their quarrel is obviously with God, confront the lie and explain the Gospel simply. In prayer, quietly and authoritatively rebuke the lie and the father of   lies - the devil. Then minister love, possibly in silence. If the person is evidently not saved, ask God if the person is ready to receive Christ.

9.   If the damage has affected other repeated experiences of their life, suggest that they face their difficulty in every situation where it arises for a time. They could ask for understanding and prayer. Eventually this will no longer be needed.

10.   If an ungodly 'soul-tie' is revealed, take authority over it in the Name of Jesus, and declare the tie broken.

Chapter 8
Just like your Mother?

"I the Lord your God am a jealous God, visiting the iniquity of the fathers on the children, on the third and the fourth generation of those who hate me." (Exodus 20:5. N.A.S.B.)

"It explains a lot!" My Vicar had just stopped over with my mother when he was on a long journey. My mother is a very strong-minded character, well-educated and articulate. She is very determined and independent. The vicar was seeing in me a reflection of her. It is true we are very alike in many ways, as many single daughters are in relation to their mothers. However, my husband disagrees and thinks I differ in several important ways.

The mother-in-law is the butt of many British jokes, and the subject of many marital bickerings. The husband is afraid that the daughter will turn out like her mother as she matures. Unfortunately we do learn our parenting from our own parents, and because we are often naturally similar in temperament, we often make the same mistakes, and this continues down the generations unless God intervenes. He can reveal and refine those abrasive traits of character and prevent or put right mistakes in parenting - all without destroying our unique personalities or violating our freewill.

The spiritual heritage also reverberates down the generations. If we have a forebear who has dabbled in spiritualist practices, who has been a member of a false cult, even seemingly innocent and socially acceptable one, then we, the descendants, can be seriously affected. Among those which are not generally recognised as cultic because they are "respectable" are New Age beliefs and practices, and membership of the Free Masons.

"It runs in the family". Sometimes a curse has been laid upon a family or a section of a family feuds or inherited negative attitudes. Descendants can be frustrated in their seeking for the Truth in Christ, and even after they have given their lives to Him, they can be inhibited in their walk with God or in seeking healing for a family genetic condition. Family ties, especially marital ties are very binding. Many parents cannot adjust to the fact that their children are independent adults. Most people find it difficult to break away from the need for approval from their parents right into late adulthood.

In ministry the source of our problems can often be traced to these generational legacies. Before any work of refining can take place, lies need to be exposed, and Truth revealed. In the case of genetic medical conditions, the curse of generations of fatalism must be refuted. Sometimes we declare that the strong family tie be broken, that the person be released to serve Christ as Lord and to grow into maturity, mentally, emotionally and spiritually.

In examining our own upbringing, and the areas that need healing in which family members had an involvement, we may realise the mistakes we are making with our children and grand-children by imitation. We are all inadequate parents, because we are all learners in the art of rearing young. But God can supply that essential wisdom and limit the damage, so that we do not perpetuate that which was inflicted upon previous members of our families.

"I should never have been born!" The young person was the result of the rape of her mother. I saw that she needed reassurance that God knew that she would be born, and wanted her to be born. She was His creation and He very much desired her friendship. Once she saw that she was treasured by God, her whole self-image was redrawn. We should all be reminded that God knows the end from the beginning, and uses even the worst events in our family history and weaves them into His purpose. We cannot change history, but God can transform the adverse consequences in our own lives, and we can be a positive influence on the future.

"From now all generations will call me blessed." (Luke 1: 50 N.I.V)
Mary was challenged to have an illegitimate child and all the shame that went with it. She was receptive and obedient to God's destiny for her; so she brought forth Jesus into the world in her generation. We can stop the tide of evil in our generation and bring forth Jesus. We do not have to be bound by the influences of previous generations; we are a new creation and unique.
"You are a chosen people…that you may declare the praises of Him who has called you out of darkness into His wonderful light." (1 Peter 2:9 N.I.V.)

Biblical case study
Abraham, Isaac and Jacob:
Breaking the chains of inheritance

"May those who curse you be cursed, and may those who bless you be blessed." *(Genesis 27:29c)*

The spoken declaration has power, as we have seen when discussing forgiveness, and never so much as in blessings and curses. The blessing of a Jewish father on his eldest son was particularly treasured; it pronounced his destiny. It was an irreversible, unbreakable oath. He was to become the patriarch with all rights of inheritance and in supreme authority over his siblings. He was to be the military and spiritual leader, the judge, the provider and the keeper of the family heritage which was then to be passed on to his eldest son.

But what if there was an error and the eldest son was by-passed? By inference he was not blessed but cursed, and would remain powerless. So it was with Isaac and his twin sons, Esau and Jacob. Isaac displayed a character which was weak and easily duped. Abraham, his father, had dominated him. As a child he had experienced the trauma of coming near to being slaughtered and offered as a sacrifice on a stone altar by his own father. Abraham had chosen his wife for him and arranged the marriage. Isaac had little say in the match, but fortunately he loved his wife. Isaac simply slipped into his father's shoes and did not have to work to make his way in the world, but inherited his father's wealth.

He even imitated Abraham's way of dealing with scary situations. Both father and son lied about their relationship to their wives when threatened. Both women were very beautiful and Abraham lied twice, once to the King of Egypt and again when he arrived in the southern part of Canaan, to King Abimelech. Then also Isaac lied to King Abimelech. Both were afraid they might be killed to allow these kings to have their wives. Each time they were found out, after the kings had taken their wives into their households. (*Genesis 12: 10-20 and Genesis 20: 1-18, then Genesis 26: 6-11*) So the sin was repeated in each generation.

Isaac was God's promised child and was favoured above his half brother Ishmael. When Abraham was seventy-five years old, God promised him that his wife Sarah, who was sixty-six years old, would bear a child who would be the father of many nations. Twenty-five years later there was still no sign of offspring and Sarah had suggested to Abraham that he help God along a bit and have a child by her handmaid, Hagar. She and Ishmael were sent into exile after Isaac was born.

The child of such elderly parents who had such a destiny on his shoulders would be necessarily fussed over, and Ishmael's rejection and disinheritance would have had a profound effect on Isaac, a weak-willed child, who grew into an ineffective parent. Again we see a repeated pattern emerging. We noted, in chapter 2, that Isaac preferred Esau, but Rebecca favoured Jacob - and so the now elderly Isaac was duped into giving the blessing of patriarchy to his younger son. We know that this was foretold by God, who also, as we have seen, understood the personality of both the sons - but the error was perpetuated in Jacob's dealings with his own sons. Isaac, when he discovered the mistake, did not have enough strength of will to stand up to his scheming wife, and Jacob got away without punishment from him.

As we noted before, Jacob, the cheat, had met with God and his character was moulded by his repeated encounters and by adversity, except in this one thing: he repeated his father's error, and paid the price, losing, apparently forever, his spoilt son, Joseph.

But God had other plans, some long-term pertaining to the destiny of the people of God, Israel. But even in this apparently adverse situation, we see redemption and the healing of the individual mind, memories and spirit, as the story of Jacob unfolds. When Jacob had learned that his son, Joseph, was alive and a ruler in Egypt, he had enough of a relationship with God to hear directly from Him. He heard God's reassurance and obeyed Him. He went down to Egypt to be reunited with his son, but also to live there in peace and prosperity for the rest of his life. The restoration of his son, gave him a renewed dignity and we found him blessing the King of Egypt as if he were his superior.

"Not that way father. This is the elder boy; put your right hand on his head." (Genesis 48:18.) So we join the story where we find Jacob, the patriarch, passing on the blessing, showing favouritism, and repeating the pattern that his father and grandfather had set. But there is a

difference for he is not deceived. He is old, but all his faculties were intact. He is in tune with God's purposes - so instead he is pronouncing God's purposes in prophecy. Jacob meets his two grandchildren, Joseph's sons, and he blesses them. In so doing, he blesses their father, but he intentionally and purposefully blesses the younger, Ephraim over the elder, Manasseh. He puts his right hand on Ephraim's head. Finally, before he dies, he pronounces blessings on all his sons, accurately prophesying the future of the twelve tribes of Israel. Truly now he is God's man!

Notes: Ministry

When taking part in prayer ministry:

1. Again, in the person's story, we need to note a repeated pattern of behaviour, personality type, and references to spiritualist or cultic practices in previous generations.
2. Pray silently for discernment and knowledge before proceeding. The real cause of the person's problems may well be hidden under the surface symptoms.
3. Excessive confusion can reveal generational spiritualist or cultic beliefs in previous generations. There is no point in arguing with a confused person. It is best to pray first and bind the evil spirits, and rebuke the lies.
4. Be alert to the revelation of strong controlling relationships in families.

5. Ministry may include the breaking of generational ties and acting this out with a piece of rope could be helpful.
6. Prayer for healing, including physical problems, may reach back into previous generations.

Chapter 9
Pots and Potential

"Whenever the pot the potter was working on turned out badly, as sometimes happens when you are working with clay, the potter would simply start again and use the same pot to make another pot."
(Jeremiah 18: 4 The Message.)

When we are babies our brains and souls are like soft clay, and very easily moulded. The Jesuits observed that if a child was trained in the ways of God for the first seven years of their lives, He would have them for life. But the clay of our minds is also very easily knocked out of shape. Our early experiences, our circumstances, the way others treat us and our own wilful sin all conspire to shape our approach to life. We have no means of defending ourselves against damage, and this is why a person practicing inner healing is so often directed to the person's early life. The tendency also is for the bruises inflicted on our persons to land on the same sensitive spot, rather as when we cut our finger it seems as if everything then conspires to irritate it and make it more sore.

So an abused person seems to attract abusers in the same sensitive area all their lives. It is a well-known sociological fact that many women who have had abusive partners do not seem to learn the lesson and often choose or are selected by successive abusive partners. It is as if the potter's wheel on which that personality is moulded has a flaw on it - maybe a sharp obtrusion -and every time the pot is recreated, it is further damaged at that particular place.

The damage may not be as obvious as overt abuse, but where in conversation a pattern of hurt emerges, or the person's manner or body language reveals discomfort when talking about similar incidents or relationships, then we can be alerted to potential root problems. Sometimes the way the person relates to us, as those who seek to understand, is revealing. A young man who recently has come to know the Lord, and whom I am trying to disciple, has revealed his inner insecurity by his evident desire to impress me as a parent figure. Whilst my acceptance of him in whatever mood, in success or failure, in anger or euphoria is, in itself, an instrument of healing, it is also indicative of his need for the parent love that only God our Father or Mother can give. Ultimately that is where he must find the deeper healing of his childhood traumatic experiences: in His relationship with the only parent that won't let him down.

"God created man in His own image." (*Genesis 1:27 A.V.)* My father was a headmaster. He told me a very upsetting story one day about a young pupil of his. She was not a high achiever and came from a dysfunctional family. In the cookery classes all the girls were asked to make a Christmas cake and decorate it. There was to be prize for the best one and pride of place in the pre-Christmas open day. This little girl was immensely proud because, after working hard and using great imagination and care, she won the first prize. The teacher suggested that they should take their cakes home to show off to

their families, then they were to return them for the great day. The little girl came back in tears. Her parents and siblings had duly admired her work of art, but when she came to collect her cake the next morning to return it to school she discovered it out of its box on the kitchen table and a large jagged piece had been cut out of it; her father had been "hungry" at supper time. My father had tears in his eyes as he related this to me.

The received understanding of the enigmatic statement in Genesis is that we are made like God. Unlike other creatures, we are spiritual beings designed for an eternal life in relationship with God. That is thankfully true, but maybe we could look at the phrase another way round. When an artist, sculptor a writer, or even a cook is preparing their work creation, they "image" what the end result will be. The creation may take some time and a lot of effort, shaping, reshaping, starting all over again sometimes like the potter. But all the time the Creator has in his mind what He wants it to look like. When God the Father of all created things, creates a male or female child, each person is "imaged" uniquely. To be 'like Jesus' is to become fully human. God wants us to be ourselves. We are not like sausages in a sausage-machine, all to be turned out the same.

Like any creator, God is immensely proud of His artistic creation. We have cultural ideas of beauty. This generation emulates the skinny figure of "Posh Spice." In certain tribes of Africa, the plumpest woman is considered the most beautiful and may become the queen! The admired personalities in this generation are the successful and assertive, but God also values the sensitive and the gentle. A "humble" person is one who depends on Him, is led by Him, who constantly refreshes his relationship with Him, whatever his natural character.

Beautiful things, in God's eyes, can be funny; take small monkeys! They can be pretty or endearingly ugly. Compare poodles and bulldogs! Beautiful things can be strong and rugged (look at elephants) or fragile, delicate and ephemeral, like mayflies. Colour, shape, size, texture, character—there is such variety in creation! "*God saw everything He had made, and indeed it was very good." (Genesis 1: 31.N.R.S.V.)*

We have seen that one definition of sin is that it is the spoiling of God's creation. God created the world in perfection, beautiful, smooth-running, with no decay or sickness, and with men and women in unbroken communication with Him, so there was no damage to their personalities. Jesus came as a man, but sinless. He is the model of what God wants each of us to be.

God knows that generally we are more sinned against than sinning. He knows what He wants us to become, and He too is desperately hurt by the damage that life and other people inflict upon His perfect image. He is very much alongside us in our pain. So He shapes our lives and brings healing to the damaged area, so that we can grow into our full potential as His sons and daughters. This process of reshaping continues all our lives and will not be fully completed until we have shed our earthly shells and meet Him face to face in our new recreated eternal bodies, in the new heaven and new earth.

"Therefore we do not lose heart. Though outwardly we are wasting away, yet inwardly we are being renewed day by day." (2 Corinthians 4: 16 N.I.V.)

Biblical case study
Zacchaeus: who was he looking for?
(Luke 19:5)

From Sunday school days we have known that Zacchaeus was a "little man." He was so small that, in his desperation to see Jesus, he climbed up into the branches of a sycamore tree as the Master passed by, and famously was asked by Him to come down and show himself.

But there was another reason, perhaps, why Zacchaeus hid in the tree: he was a hated and a vulnerable man. If caught outside it was quite possible the crowd would turn on him. He was a quisling, a tax-collector in the pay of the hated occupying forces of Rome. More than likely he also lined his pockets with excess taxes, as was the custom; after all if you are hated anyway, you might as well make a fat profit!

It does not take much imagination to see this scenario repeated in any person who is 'different', in any society. The 'fat' boy, the girl who is underdeveloped, the child with a purple birth mark on their face, the one whose clothes are ill-fitting, never clean or just not fashionable 'designer' style. All these children are likely to be very self-conscious and picked on or ridiculed by their school contemporaries.

When I lived in a run-down housing estate near the school where I taught, it came to my notice that one of our neighbour's sons was severely neglected. His clothes were over-large cast-offs. He was unkempt, 'nitty' and grubby. He was cruelly teased by his class-mates. He rarely had any breakfast and his only meal of the day was his free school lunch.

In the holidays he came and ate with my children. He came on holiday with us too. But the biggest breakthrough with him came when I finally persuaded the school nurse to treat his nits, and identify a clean, second-hand school uniform which fitted him and provide him with underwear and some sports kit. He started to hold his head higher from that day onwards. He cleaned himself up.

Another Christian lady also took him under her wing and added to his self-confidence with a very long-term commitment to him. She followed every detail of his career after he finally left school to enter into the army, and became the smartest young private on the block! Some people had believed in him and given him a new start.

Many people in later life often demonstrate their sense of rejection by either becoming very withdrawn or by being uncomfortably, noisily assertive. (Adolf Hitler could possibly be a good example). I suggest that maybe

Zacchaeus was compensating for his small size and decided that, if he was rejected by society, he had nothing to lose anyway. Being rich, even by cheating, and being notorious and isolated became his comfort zone.

His immediate decision to respond to Jesus' invitation was a courageous one. Jesus asked him not only to come down from the tree and expose himself to the watching crowd, but also showed that he would like to sample Zacchaeus' no doubt sumptuous hospitality. He heard his name being called. Jesus knew who he was! The fact that Jesus, this great Rabbi of whom he had heard but who he had not been able to see, was willing to accept him publicly, made all the difference to his self-image and prompted his instant response. He was considered worthy of attention, and Jesus' open demonstration of acceptance, His love in action, caused him to repent, give away half his wealth, and repay anyone he had cheated. Zacchaeus not only found Jesus - he found himself, the man made in the image of God.

Notes: Ministry

When taking part in prayer ministry:

1. Keep in mind that what we call 'sin' may well be a reaction to emotional pain in an individual. They are still responsible for their reactions, but often sheer will-power to overcome is not enough. What they need is healing.
2. Note the clues---the patterns of behaviour and repeated attitudes in relationships.

3.   Rejection is a common emotional trauma, and once identified might take a long-term accepting relationship to address it. The Gospel of the unconditional love of God is a powerful antidote, especially lived out in the lives of those who minister, including us.

4.   As we pray for these damaged people, we can ask God to allow us to see the potential, the completed image of what they were intended to be, and bring hope to those struggling with incomplete personalities.

Chapter 10
Stones and Rocks

"The stones with which the Temple was built had been prepared at the quarry, so that there was no noise made by hammers, axes, or any other iron tools as the Temple was being built." (*1Kings 6:7*)

We, individually and as members of Christ's church, are the Temple of the Holy Spirit – (*1 Corinthians 3:16*. Note: in the Greek, *"you"* in this verse is plural). We are rough stones which need shaping: the sharp corners need to be knocked off! The Lord takes such trouble over each one, preparing us, if we allow Him to, away from the site of ministry in the Temple, to ensure that there is no friction when we are fitted into place. As we submit our lives to the Holy Spirit, we give Him the right to proceed with this often painful preparation for His service. He is committed to making sure that we are ready before we can fully be of service to Him. If we attempt to minister in the Temple before we have been prepared we are in danger of causing mayhem.

Lack of preparation, the unwillingness to allow the Lord to identify our weaknesses, trim our hang-ups and heal our character flaws is, I believe, one of the greatest hindrances to the work of God in our churches. God the Holy Spirit is ready, like a stone mason, to take His craftsman's hammer. He finds just the right fault line in our characters and with great skill taps gently at that spot. Piece by piece chunks of our encrusted past fall away. In doing so He prepares us to fit snugly into the wall of his great Temple in the place where He needs us.

He hasn't finished yet though, as underneath the crusts of dirt hardened by life's experiences lies a diamond. It still needs delicate detailed cutting and polishing by the Master jeweller until it shines with the reflected light of the glory of God. A diamond has many faces; together they glitter so brightly that possibly the individual face may be obscured, but yet each facet has a part to play. *"All of us then reflect the glory of the Lord with uncovered faces."* *(2 Corinthians 3:18.)* The Holy Spirit's "hammer" operates as some or all of these:

1. **The Word.**
   "Is not my Word like a fire? says the Lord, and like a hammer that breaks the rocks in pieces?" *(Jeremiah 23:29 N.R.S.V.)* A specific scripture may directly address our weakness.

2. **Other people.**
   We are like stones in a river. We knock the corners off each other!

3. **Circumstances.**
   God often allows circumstances which are upsetting at the time to reveal our need for change in certain areas. For example beware asking for "more patience". My experience informs me that very soon circumstances will arise which will stretch my patience or underline my lack of it!

4. **Significant events replayed, revisited and recreated in His presence**.
   Sometimes these are revived memories, provoked by some experience. They can be surfaced by the

Holy Spirit. When Jesus is allowed into the painful memory, His presence, attitude and words bring healing.

We have seen how many of these have been used in the Biblical case studies we have already examined. In the shaping of Simon Peter, however, each is clearly exemplified.

Biblical Case Study:
Simon Peter - the shaping of a rock

"Simon, son of John, do you love Me?" (John 21:16)

On this occasion, after His resurrection when he met Peter on the beach, Jesus challenged his impetuous disciple three times with similar words. Peter had been taken on a long and sometimes painful journey to reach this point. Jesus sees his potential in character and gifts, and wants to use him mightily to kick start the new order of the Kingdom of God. Jesus will soon be leaving His disciples to return to heaven. He will leave His followers to continue what He started, and needs to ensure that this rock is shaped and ready for use.

The process of healing in Peter's life is fascinating to observe. Jesus was not rubbing salt into the wound when He asked these questions. He was simply being direct, getting to the heart of the matter, making Peter face himself and declare his heart. Jesus already knew Peter's heart. It was Peter who was bewildered and confused about himself. It was he who needed to find out and confess his renewed commitment.

The three challenges will resonate with Peter, to counteract the three denials torturing his conscience. Outside the courtroom where Jesus' trial was conducted, he declared three times when challenged that he did not know Jesus. The crowing of a cock, as Jesus predicted, and Jesus' look of compassionate disappointment compounded his shame. There is no record of Peter's presence at the cross to see his master crucified, and he only reappears in the narrative when he receives a report from the women that Jesus had been raised from the dead. He rushed to the tomb in high anticipation, he overtook the other more cautious disciples at the tomb entrance, and characteristically burst in. Maybe, just maybe, he might have an opportunity to make amends for his shameful behaviour! Hope was revived when he saw the linen clothes lying as if Jesus' body had passed through, but Jesus' resurrection was not confirmed until he met him on the beach.

John's record of this conversation very carefully records details of the Greek words used *(John 21:15-17)*. Jesus questions Peter the first time: *"Do you love me more than these?"* He uses the word for love, in Greek, *"agape"*, which is the divine quality; self-emptying, sacrificial, unconditional love. Peter replies: *"Lord You know that I love You."* The word he uses for love, *"phileo"*, means friendship, loyalty or brotherly affection. It is not as strong. It could be that Peter, so shaken by his former infidelity, is shy of using the divine word, but also he may be trying to convey his renewed loyalty.

In the second challenge: *"Do you love Me?"* Jesus again here uses the word *"agape"* – unconditional love. Peter replies as before, with *"phileo"* love. Then, on the third challenge Jesus says again: *"Do you love Me?"*
But He now used the word *"phileo"* for love, as if He is saying (and some translations include this emphasis) *"Do you even have loyalty for Me?"* (Living Bible)

At this Peter is upset, He replies: *"Lord, You know everything, You know that I love (phileo) you!"* Something else has happened to restore Peter, to heal his pain of disloyalty. They both know it and he is changed forever.
Jesus could now commission him: *"Take care of My sheep."*
Peter, as we know, goes on to be a pillar of the church - the disciple who at Pentecost stood up before a vast crowd, preached about the risen Lord, and saw three thousand people converted in a single day. He took authority and commanded many healings in Jesus' name, and was able, a simple fisherman to enter dialogue with the trained theologian, Paul, and prevail in the argument. The man who had been a religious zealot, always right, had become a humble channel of God's power.

The process was long and complicated, because on the surface Peter was a loyal and committed follower of Jesus. But he was volatile and often spoke before his brain was engaged! We love him because he was so prone to put his big foot in it, just like many of us! Deeper

106

than that, Peter was confident in his own ability to stay the course through thick and thin. Jesus is going to have to put him through severe lessons to turn that self-reliance into humble dependence through faith in God.

We do not know what seeds were sown in Peter's early life to make him the man that he was. Maybe his character is sourced in nature - formed by birth and inheritance, rather than nurture - formed by experience. All we know is that he bursts upon the scene as a tough, apparently self-confident fisherman. He had observed Jesus in action for some time in Capernaum. He must have heard Him teach, seen Him cast out many demons and heal many sick people *(Luke 4: 31f)*. Jesus had been to Simon's house and Simon had witnessed the instant healing of his mother-in-law, who had a high fever. Simon had chance to ponder the identity of Jesus. His actions are not as impetuous as they appeared for he was ready to respond when Jesus appeared on the beach *(Luke 5:1-11)*.

Peter obeyed Jesus, but he was dubious when they pushed the boats out to resume fishing during the day, protesting that they had had a fruitless night. They made a huge catch and afterwards Peter fell on his knees before Jesus and made that significant declaration: "*Go away from me, Lord! I am a sinful man!*" *(Luke 5:8)* It demonstrated his deep conviction of his own need and Jesus' claim upon his life. Jesus had met him and his fishing companions at the point of their need. They had caught no fish. Jesus' word of knowledge and advice, and their obedience, produced an over-abundant result. They had an early lesson in insight and provision!

They all made an instant commitment, and abandoned their way of life for three and a half years, until Jesus died. Jesus proceeded to teach them patiently and released them into His ministry of prayer, healing, deliverance and dependence on God. Jesus demonstrated His exemplary skills as a Teacher in the style of a Jewish Rabbi:

1) He instructed His disciples from His superior knowledge and illustrated by His own example, and by familiar visual aids.
2) He asked questions and corrected wrong concepts.
3) He sent them out to practical situations. Sometimes they passed these tests; at other times they failed and He patiently corrected them and demonstrated the way of doing the task that His Father had taught Him through the Holy Spirit.
4) He recapped each point where they had shown weakness, then retested.
5) Once they had passed the more advanced test, He set others later to make sure they had retained the understanding.
6) Finally he set them to teach others - but only when He was sure they were ready.

Jesus did a thorough job of reshaping Peter before He deemed him ready to lead. We, His disciples, cannot afford to take any short-cuts either, especially if we are called into leadership.

Notes: Ministry

When taking part in prayer ministry:

1. If someone is telling a "hard luck" story, we need to be particularly sensitive to God's leading, asking for wisdom and knowledge. It is very easy to misinterpret God's dealings in the situation.
2. Be alert as to where possibly God is dealing with flaws of character in them. Maybe the question would then be: "What have you learned from all of this?"
3. We need to listen and note the emotions as people relate their stories.
4. Is there self-pity or resentment? Is there acceptance in the midst of puzzlement? Is there deep hurt, loss or bereavement? In which case our ministry is comfort and reassurance of God's love.

Chapter 11
Metamorphosis

"Be not conformed to this world;, but be transformed by the renewing of your mind, that you may prove what is the acceptable and perfect will of God." (Romans 12:2 A.V.)

The word "transformed" in New Testament Greek is "*metamorphosis*". This is a familiar word in biology and geology indicating the total structural change in the substance of a living creature or rock. A metamorphic rock is one that has been subjected to such heat and pressure that it has melted down into molten minerals, some of which have separated out. When the rock cools and solidifies, these minerals remain distinct. Seams of metals and precious stones are located in these rocks. Diamonds are produced by such a process.

Some of us need excessive heat and pressure to reform our minds. We are so steeped in the values and mindset of the world or received religious mores, that we require radical transformation. Note that the verbs are passive "*Be transformed*". This is not something we do ourselves. We would not be able to. God arranges circumstances in such a way that we face our false concepts, and His love transforms them.

Often Christians set false standards and goals for themselves, then are bewildered when God does not cooperate with them, or give them strength to abide by their rules of living. It is at this point that we learn that

God's ways are often not our ways, and learn lessons that we may not learn in any other way. It is a process of discovering the mercy and grace of God in the midst of what we see as failure.

It may shock some readers to learn that I experienced such a transformation in my thinking through the heat and pressure of a divorce. I had been a Christian for about ten years, and I understood the binding nature of the marriage vow. If I had been a friend of someone in my position, I would have been shocked and dismissive and would have been vociferously against even the contemplation of divorce. In my mind God would reject me if I broke this law.

My husband was a spirit-filled Christian but mentally ill. He had schizophrenia, which was compounded by the activity of demons in his life. As a Christian he had used spiritualist methods to get his own way in a situation. This had left a legacy of lies in his mind, and he seemed unwilling or unable to address his spiritual problems. As I have already explained, I experienced five years of abuse, the details of which I am not going to disclose. We had three little children, and the situation came to a head when I recognised the interference of demons in the violence of a mental breakdown.

It took me about a year to realise that he was resisting the opportunity to be delivered and healed. We were living in a Christian community by then and he had every opportunity for compassionate ministry. With the support of the community, I still worked very hard to try to make the marriage work, but it was very one-sided, and my patience frequently ran out. There were times when depression nearly overcame me, I felt trapped and hopeless.

The community also allowed me to witness similar situations amongst those families who lived in such close proximity. I observed a family who had stayed together, even though the husband was controlling and abusive. Watching the wife especially who had suffered so much psychologically that she was unable to express her own viewpoint or personality, I realised that for my own sanity and for the sake of our three children, I would have to take action. My husband was still ill, although controlled by drugs, and we agreed that he should go to stay with his parents for an indefinite period while I prayed and considered our future together.

It took me two years to come to terms with the fact that I had failed to hold the marriage together; I was reduced to bewilderment and shame. A number of factors led me to make the decision for legal separation, then divorce. Having made the decision, mostly for the sake of our children who needed at least one sane parent, I stuck to it. The worst I could do for my husband was to waver. He needed to know where he stood. He was, after all, a very sick man who could not cope with responsibility.

On the day of the hearing at court, I experienced a miracle of timing which prevented my having to make any statement in public about my husband's behaviour, and I walked out with a "decree nisi" after about twenty minutes. (Two years later my husband died very suddenly from a heart attack.) That day I learned the extent of the grace of God. He loved me as I was, understood everything about my decision, and most of all had laid aside my own concept of His standards. He is my Protector, Counsellor and Redeemer. In this I received a healing of mind and emotions which was continued when I met and married my second husband, whose personality, approach to marriage and parenthood, and whose steadfast love countered all the trauma of the former relationship.

This metamorphosis in my thinking produced a compassion for people who are in trouble, made me see that God does not work with hard and fast rules, but allows for our weaknesses. He takes the basic material of our beings and transforms it into something which reflects His compassion so that He can use us in His kingdom. *"As the heavens are higher than the earth, so are My ways higher than yours ways."* *(Isaiah 55:9a N.I.V.)*

Biblical Case Study:
Peter: melted down and reconstructed

Simon (renamed later as Peter) was a natural leader, and as such needed concentrated training. Jesus treatment of him was radical and at times severe. He needed the process of metamorphosis to transform his most hardened concepts. His most prominent fault was his self-appointed role as the spokesman for the disciples and his tendency to blurt out comments without thinking.

He revealed his heart and insight when Jesus asked the disciples who they thought He was. *"Simon Peter answered: 'You are the Messiah, the Son of the living God.'" (Matthew 16:16)*

This is when Jesus changes Simon's name to Peter, meaning a rock, and declares that his confession will be the foundation of the church. He is also implying that Peter, through his faith, will be the solid reliable leader. He gives him His authority to access the powers of the Kingdom of Heaven, and change the face of the world.

But Jesus then tests Peter and the disciples, by foretelling His own suffering and death, as the Messiah. The popular Jewish concept of the Messiah was that He would come and change the political situation, and as a warrior drive out the oppressors of Israel. The idea of a vulnerable Saviour who would give up His life for sinners was anathema to them. Peter remonstrates with Him as he cannot bear to imagine Jesus leaving them. Jesus retorts sharply that Peter's thoughts are sourced in Satan's world view. Peter certainly, still has a lot to learn!

Peter is also one of the inner circle of three disciples who are chosen to witness Jesus' transfiguration, but in the midst of this awesome experience, Peter again demonstrates his inability to keep his mouth shut, and babbles almost meaningless suggestions about putting up tents for Jesus and His two visitors, Moses and Elijah. Possibly this is an attempt to freeze the experience in time so that the everyday world is kept at bay for longer *(Luke 17:4).*

"Simon, Simon! Listen! Satan has received permission to test all of you, to separate the good from the bad, as a farmer separates the wheat from the chaff. But I have prayed for you, Simon that your faith will not fail. And when you turn back to Me, you must strengthen your brothers." (*Luke 22:31*.) Significantly Jesus uses the name Simon here. He knows Simon's fatal flaw and knows he will fall at the last hurdle. The disciples have just been quarrelling about who should be the greatest in the Kingdom of heaven. Peter, no doubt, was making a vociferous claim! But Jesus is careful to point out that in the Kingdom of God values are turned on their head; the roles of master and slave are reversed: the leader is the servant.

Peter, of course, protests at Jesus' prediction that He will suffer and die and that Peter would deny he knew Jesus. He is still full of bluster and self-confidence - sure that he, at least, will not let Jesus down. But Jesus knows better. Significantly, also He does not pray for Peter's endurance but for his faith. Peter has to fail in order to break his fixed understanding of where his strength for service lies.

At first, when Jesus was arrested in the Garden of Gethsemane, Peter's courage and tenacity were not in question. He took a sword and cut off one of the High Priest's slave's ear. He was eager to defend his Lord, and it is evident that he still did not understand Jesus' destiny to submit to death. We can almost hear Jesus' "Tut, tut!" as He heals the ear and rebukes Peter again, patiently reminding him that He must do what God has asked of Him.

Peter then, after this, was still one of the two disciples brave enough to follow Jesus to the judgement hall, although he hovered outside until he was brought in by his companion. Then, of course, his nerve failed him, and he made an ignominious retreat weeping bitterly. Peter's self-confidence was now in tatters, his self-imposed standard of behaviour violated. Here is the point of metamorphosis. The former mind-set was in melt-down under the pressure.

The healing of this memory and Peter's restoration to faith is a model of Jesus' gracious dealings with those who whole-heartedly seek to follow Him and allow Him to shape their personalities and teach them total dependence on Him. It began with a glimmer of hope for Peter. Sometimes a single word from Jesus can change our perception: *"Now go and give this message to his disciples, and Peter…"* (Mark *16:7* N.I.V). The speaker is an angel at Jesus' tomb after He was raised from the dead, commissioning the women to spread the good news.

Jesus still wanted to see him and talk to him! The disciples were all there in the room with a locked door, when Jesus visited them in His risen body. There is no record of Peter's reaction to this, but even though Jesus had given evidence of God's power over death and so His claim to be the sinless Son of God, Peter was still the disciple who decided to return to his old life, possibly because of his painful sense of failure. It is here, at the place where Peter started, that Jesus brings about his deep healing. *"Because the Lord disciplines those whom He loves." (Hebrews 12:6 N.I.V.)*

Notes: Ministry

When taking part in prayer ministry:

1. As people tell their stories it is vital that we remain "unshockable".
   Unless we have walked where they have walked, we cannot appreciate their situation or God's dealings with them.
2. Even if we suspect that God is using adverse circumstances to address the person's weakness, we must be careful not to compound their sense of failure. We can point out that God deals most severely with those who have potential in discipleship and that hardship is the compliment of God who trusts that we will not deny His love, and eventually become stronger because of the trials of our faith.

Chapter 12
Action Replay in the Company of Jesus

The word of knowledge was such a strange picture that I was reluctant to share it. I seemed to be lying on my back looking up at a greeny-blue, shimmering, bubbly surface above my head: a transparent tent, perhaps? I asked Jim (not his real name) if he'd been camping as a child; no recollection. I explored other possibilities, and then felt the nudge just to go for it! When I finally described my picture, Jim recognised it immediately.

Of course! He told his story. He recalled when he was in his mid-teens lying at the bottom of his local swimming pool looking up helplessly, ready to drown. It was his best friend, Ben, (also not his real name) who was a couple of years older than him who spotted him and effected his rescue from this watery grave. He was resuscitated and was none the worse for his ordeal.

But Ben was also his hero, his mentor. He had become like his older brother, the one on whom he modelled his life - the leader, the inspiration, his encourager. A couple of years after the swimming-pool incident, Ben died suddenly, and the massive loss compounded the trauma of the near-drowning experience. Jim found relationships difficult. In particular he could not receive in his heart the concept of Jesus being his friend who would *'never leave him'.(Hebrews 13:5)* Although Jim has a powerful prophetic ministry where he is required to go out on a limb for the Word and insight he is given by the Holy Spirit, he was insecure and fretful in many situations.

118

Gently and carefully I suggested to Jim that together we should return in his imagination to the swimming-pool, then afterwards to the situation where Jim was when he heard of Ben's death, and ask Jesus to make Himself known by His presence right there with him. I pointed out that God understands our concept of history and linear time, but He Himself is not in time. To Him all events happen in the "Now". It is as if our life time-line is held, not horizontally but vertically, and He looks down from above and all the life events are stacked on top of each other. So He was there, at the swimming-pool, and subsequently when Jim heard the news of his friend's death.

When he was ready, we did this, and the emotions of those moments surfaced in Jim's mind and heart. He wept out his fear and his grief, then together we saw and heard the words of Jesus who was there with Him, watching over His precious child so that he did not drown, weeping with Him, bringing words of comfort, reassurance and peace. I then prayed for the renewing of Jim's memories, not that he should forget, but that the brain cells which stored those memories might be modified, and his recall would be one of knowledge of protection and of sweet recollection of his time with Ben. Jim faced the world with renewed courage and restored his relationship with His Lord who is his "*Friend who sticks closer than a brother." (Proverbs 18:24.N.A.S.B.)*

This was one of many times that I have witnessed the living ministry of our compassionate Lord Jesus into individual past histories. Memories, even forgotten ones, can surface by a word of knowledge as we have seen. When we are asleep, our conscious mind which suppresses memory is switched off, and memories and their associate emotions enter our dreams. This is not the place to discuss the interpretation of dreams. That is a book in itself, but suffice it to say that often the elements of dreams reveal our true attitudes. The minister's primary question, if the person who is disturbed has experienced a dream is to ask what emotions accompanied it, and this can be a key to the memory which requires healing. Memories can also be triggered by a sight, a sound, especially evocative music, the taste of something and the most enduring - the sense of smell.

A group of young people stayed once with me in an outdoor centre which had a wood-burning open fire. My daughter was quite young, and one evening as she sat with me alone, on my lap for a cuddle, by the fire, she started suddenly to talk about her father who was by then dead. I realised that the smell had triggered her memory, as we had a wood-burning fire in our home when she was a small child, and for the first time she expressed her real feelings about her Dad, and we were able to face them and she experienced a healing.

Jesus is not restricted by time. He can enable us to revisit past events with Him beside us, speaking words of comfort and encouragement, transforming the memory. This can be ministered in a number of ways. Each person is unique and our job is to introduce Jesus into a situation and let Him do the work. As in imagination, the Holy Spirit renews the painful occasion of the memory, through a word of knowledge as above, through a dream, or simply through talking about it. We walk together into the memory and see Jesus standing there. Often a prophetic word from the person ministering reflects Jesus' compassionate involvement - always present, always hurting with us, always reassuring with words of comfort and encouragement.

Recently, I witnessed Jesus ministering this without any human intervention. I suggested to the small group of four people that they recalled their most painful early memory. None of them disclosed these. All I did as minister was ask Jesus to be with them in the situation, and in the silence that followed He did His gentle work of healing and restoration. Two young women faced their traumas, took Jesus into their painful memories and reported a great sense of peace and joy afterwards which endured.

We saw the effect of an "action replay" in the story of Joseph when his brothers finally fulfilled his dream and bowed before him. The pattern is clearly depicted in the way that Jesus ministers the deeper healing of Simon Peter, the eager disciple of Jesus, as we shall see.

Biblical Case Study:
Peter: the rough diamond polished

"When Peter heard that it was the Lord, he wrapped his outer garment round him (for he had taken his clothes off), and jumped into the water." (John 21:7)

It is no accident that John records this second miracle of the catch of fish after Jesus' resurrection. This is no mistake of chronology, as some commentators argue. It is an action replay for a purpose. Like the first time, Jesus called out to the fishermen who have toiled all night and caught nothing. He told them where to throw the net out and they caught one hundred and fifty-three fishes in one haul! Peter could not contain himself for joy; the message to him was so obvious. Jesus was taking him back to the scene where he first met the Lord, confessed his sin, was forgiven and left everything to follow this amazing Man. It reminded him of the generosity, overflowing provision, insight and miracle power that had first attracted him to Jesus.

So he repeated his action of running towards Jesus, even if it meant he got rather wet! Then Jesus did something which characterised His ministry, He served them Himself. It was a simple barbeque breakfast on the beach - fresh fish and bread. Without doubt, no food ever tasted better to Peter. He was restored into Jesus' friendship. He could relax. Jesus made much of shared meals, both in His teachings and practice. Through them, He expressed His family relationship, His companionship, His enjoyment of the simple pleasures of human life. Life is good in His company. Peter had returned to his first love.

Then followed the challenges about love which we have examined. Peter was not on the defensive here. He had experienced his acceptance by his beloved Master. He knew that Jesus also accepted that Peter was humbled - longer bragging and not yet ready to claim *agape*, unconditional, sacrificial love. All the same, he was affirming that he was loyal to the One who loved him enough not only to forgive him and to give him an important job to do. He was learning that leadership is servanthood.

Jesus then prophesied into the future. For Him the main battle for Peter's mind, heart and trust was over. Jesus referred back to his previous approach to life: *"When you were young you used to get ready and go anywhere you wanted to…"* In other words he was self-willed and independent. *"But when you are old, you will stretch out your hands and someone else will bind you and take you where you don't want to go." (John 21:18)*. John comments that this predicts the manner in which Peter will die (traditionally he was crucified upside-down) but equally it could just mean that Peter had a lesson in dependence on Jesus leading, and interdependence with Jesus' other followers. *"Then Jesus said to him, 'Follow Me.'" (John21:19)*.

A flash of the old Peter appears after this. He becomes positively nosy about what was to happen to John. Possibly because John was so close to Jesus (he was known as the beloved disciple) Peter thought he would be more privileged. Jesus tells Peter in effect to mind his own business. Peter's job was to follow Him. Each disciple has to be brought to a position where he is willing to go and remain where Jesus places him, or there will be a gap in the Body of Christ, a missing limb or organ, and the overall ministry will be weakened.

Jesus' greatest desire is that we should be in close relationship with Him, that is why He is so committed to shaping the rocks. As we have seen it can be a painful process given the raw material, but there is glory in the end product. By this awesome act of recreation and healing, Jesus had polished the faces of His precious diamond that was Peter, until they shone, reflecting the brilliance of Jesus Himself.

Notes: Ministry

When taking part in prayer ministry:

1. Note in the person's story if they refer to something which reminds them of the original trauma.
2. In ministry, we can lead the person in imagination back into the past trauma. We see Jesus as present in that situation and ask Him to bring comfort and speak to the person. This can be left to Him, or given as a word of wisdom by the minister as they are led.

3. This can be reapplied, if necessary, on the same occasion to other traumas in the person's life. Often if the key hurt has been identified, this is not necessary.
4. With mature, prayerful Christians, they can be encouraged to address other traumas themselves without the further intervention of a minister.

Chapter 13
A Word in your Ear

"He sent forth His Word and healed them." (Psalm 107:20 N.I.V)

There are two words in the New Testament for the 'Word of God' – *"logos"* and *"rhema"*. The *"logos"* is the generalised Word of God, the Truth contained in the Bible, while the *"rhema"* is the particular Word of God which the Holy Spirit specifically applies to a situation or person. It is to be treasured and it gives encouragement, comfort and direction to our lives.

It can come to us various ways - sometimes in a clear, unmistakable phrase in words we understand, but also through the *"logos"* Word as we read it for ourselves, or listen to others. It can be given by a third party as a prophetic word or word of knowledge. God often speaks a *"rhema"* Word into our lives if we are ready to listen. This Word can be a beginning of healing in itself.

A young woman, a very new Christian, recently attended a small group who were considering how memories affect the way we conduct our lives, and specifically our walk with God. As she recalled a significant memory, she called to mind her grandmother who had been the symbol of security in her life and had died a few years ago. She had never really been able to come to terms with this loss, and deeply desired to see her grandmother and talk with her 'at least once'. She always in times of stress recalled her affection and 'talked' to her grandmother about her troubles.

In this session she realised that her greatest fear was being abandoned. The leader did not require her to share this memory, but simply suggested that they all prayed together in silence, but asking Jesus to speak to them. In the time we waited in silence, facing squarely an incident which produced the fear, she saw a figure she knew to be Jesus come into the room of the memory, and heard Him speak. She knew it was His voice, (and she said it was not my voice). He said to her, "I will never leave you."

It wasn't until several weeks later that she recounted this experience, and realised that she had been substituting her attachment to her grandmother for a relationship with God. As she renounced these efforts to contact her grandmother, who had died, she then received assurance of the Lord's constancy in all circumstances of life. This led to a process of healing and a closeness to the Lord which is still continuing. This desire to hold on to former symbols of security especially in close relationships is what often (but not in this case), causes people to seek spiritualist mediums and abandon their faith as the false manifestation appears. In the story of King Saul we see this exemplified.

Saul: impressive but spiritually deaf

"Saul, an impressive young man without equal among the Israelites—a head taller than any of the others." (1 Samuel 9: 2 N.I.V)

Judging by his appearance, Saul was the kind of king that Israel desired - a warrior. Through the prophet Samuel, the Lord had warned the people that appointing a king might create more problems than it solved. However their request prevailed and Samuel identified Saul and anointed him as king. They looked for outward human strengths, rather than maturity and spiritual qualities. But Samuel's choice was confirmed as Saul received the gift of prophecy through the Holy Spirit. Samuel, the prophet gave Saul his *"rhema"* Word. He told him that he was to… *"Do whatever your hand finds to do, for God is with you." (1 Samuel 10: 7 N.I.V.).* It was further confirmed by the tribes who gathered together to select a king: they too, chose Saul.

Saul was elected, anointed by God, given gifts and commissioned: but it wasn't enough. He had an underlying character flaw which needed identifying and correcting. But he missed many opportunities, times of crisis where he faced his need and turned away to his own solution, rather than listening to and being led by the voice of God.

We are not told the source of Saul's weak character. It does appear that he was easily influenced by others, afraid of what people would say. This pattern was repeated as his story unfolds. His father seemed to treat him as no more than a servant and sent him to search for lost donkeys (*1 Samuel 9:3*). Possibly this kind of relationship with his father coloured his understanding of his relationship with God who called him into His service. Saul seemed at a loss when the donkeys could not be found, and was directed by the servant who had been sent with him. The future king appeared to lack initiative and the ability to plan ahead. Paradoxically, it was this incident which initially lead him to Samuel. When it came time to present him to the tribes of Israel as their chosen king, he mysteriously disappeared. He was found hiding away from the public eye. He appeared self-conscious and bashful - a form of pride in which a person does not want to be exposed for what he is.

He was not popular with everyone, and he knew it. God was with him and when he was stirred to anger and ready to lead his people into his first battle against their traditional enemy, the Ammonites, he was able to rally a mighty army (*1 Samuel 11*). But it is indicative of his insecurity that, rather than relying upon the Lord who had clearly chosen him to be their leader, he used threats to provoke their loyalty and relied on Samuel's name to increase his credibility. He did win that first battle, and was established in his place of authority. His charisma, at the outset, united the nation in their struggle against their enemies.

This affirmation was not enough to counter Saul's sense of inferiority for he had not made a deep relationship of his own with God. He relied on Samuel to give spiritual leadership. Although he had experienced the Holy Spirit, because of his weakness, he mixed his motivations with what his natural being desired and exercised his own will. He failed at the first test of his faith. His understanding was limited. Even though he had been told that God was with him, he could not trust in the face of crisis. He wanted to earn the Lord's favour by a sacrifice. When he assumed that Samuel had let him down by delaying to come to make a sacrifice and when the Philistines were assembled in huge numbers to fight the Israelites, fear of failure caused him to make the burnt offering himself, and he earned Samuel's fatal rebuke when he did at last arrive and see what Saul had done.

God was not interested in the sacrifice at all. This would be a religious act rather than an act of faith. Saul could have inspired his cowardly scattering troops and gone into battle and prevailed, basing his boldness on the word of God already revealed to him. God wanted a "*man after his own heart*"
(*1 Samuel 13:14 N.R.S.V.*). Instead this was a leader who listened to the lies and fears of his own heart. At this point Samuel realised that Saul was not ready to face his own weakness and had not responded in obedience to the "*rhema*" Word of God which had been offered to bring about his healing and make him a fit leader of men. Samuel saw that the kingdom under Saul would *"not endure". (1 Samuel 13:14a N.I.V.)*

From then on we see the steady decline of Saul. He still won some battles, mostly due to the loyalty of his army and specifically his son. However, he made many unwise decisions, not based on faith, but as before on rules and the superstitious use of religious ritual. He began to make hasty judgements and gave rash orders. Saul enquired of God before he went into battle again against the Philistines, but God gave him no answer. Saul had previously required his army to fast until he had defeated the Philistines. He made a vow and cursed anyone who broke his religious rule.

Curses, by the people of God, are powerful and put them in alliance with evil powers. Saul, in this action, was opening the doors to his own destruction. From then on he was plagued by satanic influences. Jonathan, his son, was a hero to the army. With the help of only his armour bearer, he had recently won a skirmish against the Philistines. He had been hungry and had eaten some honey which restored his strength. His father tried to make him the scapegoat for God's silence about the outcome of the battle and ordered his execution. Saul was overruled by his own soldiers.

Again Saul through Samuel was given a "*rhema*" word (*1 Samuel 15*). He was to attack the Amalekites. This tribe had attacked the Israelites as they travelled from Egypt to the Promised Land. The powers of hell did all they could to discourage and bring down the newly fledged people of God. These Amalekites were descendants of Esau, symbols of the fleshly appetites. Now Saul was required to utterly destroy this enemy – man, woman and child - and to take no spoils of battle in the form of any living thing.

This seems like a harsh and bloody command by God, but it demonstrates how well God knew Saul. In His mercy, He realised that if Saul rescued any plunder, in the form of slaves or meat, Saul and his army would be tempted to indulge themselves, and would again lose their spiritual edge. Saul won the battle but did not destroy Agag their king, and plundered the best of the livestock for a victory feast. Samuel challenged him about this and he compounded his disobedience with a lie. He claimed, very piously, that, of course, he was going to sacrifice the animals in thanks to God for his victory.

Samuel was not fooled and he spoke with insight into Saul's motives: *"To obey is better than to sacrifice—for rebellion is like the sin of divination, and arrogance like the evil of idolatry." (1 Samuel 15:22c+23a N.I.V.).* What he is saying is that Saul is substituting religion for any real relationship with God. He is covering up his lust for meat, his own weak judgement and resolve, and his fear of the people, *(1 Samuel 15: 24.)* Samuel responds by ordering Agag's execution, and finishing the job which Saul had neglected.

Surely this is the most cogent object lesson for those who seek leadership of God's people and those who seek to minister in the gifts of the Holy Spirit? God gives those gifts freely, but if we do not address our inner weaknesses and take the healing offered, our lives and the work of God's Kingdom can be shipwrecked.

Samuel knew this of Saul, who understood too late and sought repentance but Samuel answered: *"The Lord has torn the kingdom of Israel from you, and has given it to one of your neighbours - to one better then you." (1 Samuel 15:28).* He meant David, of course, who succeeded Saul as king, but was 'better', not necessarily in behaviour, and his life had its very immoral moments. But David trusted the goodness of God and recognised that He wanted his cooperation in building the Kingdom of God. He listened to the Word and commands of God, and sought to believe and obey them.

Samuel sought David out and anointed him to be the future king in Saul's place. *"The Lord's spirit left Saul, and an evil spirit sent by the Lord tormented him." (1 Samuel 16:14).* Saul when he was tormented by an evil spirit, was encouraged to invite David into his court, first as a musician to soothe him when he was depressed and agitated. Then David, in the power of his anointing, defeated the Philistine giant Goliath, and afterwards was successful in several military encounters. The adulation by the common people that greeted him as he returned from battle provoked Saul's jealousy, and the next time David was summonsed to play music to soothe him, Saul suddenly went mad and tried to kill him. The evil spirit had taken him over, exploiting a fault-line of weakness in Saul's character to enter and take control.

Saul spent much of the rest of his reign persecuting David, once he realised that God had chosen him to rule in his place. He pursued him and sought his death. He had once loved David. He had now been bereaved of that friendship, recognised that he had lost his kingdom, had lost sight of who he was, and worst of all had lost his relationship with God. He was about to slide into the abyss.

Notes: Ministry

When taking part in prayer ministry:

1. The *"rhema"* word: as God leads us we need to adhere to His revelation through this special word.
2. The word often comes in the form of encouragement, but at other times it may be stringent, and it takes courage to speak out a word of warning.
3. Again repeated patterns of behaviour may indicate a weakness of character which could potentially end in the downfall even of a Spirit-filled person.

Chapter 14
Vessels Cleansed and Refilled

"For if a demon leaves, it goes into the deserts for a while, seeking rest and finding none. Then it says: 'I will return to the man I came from.' So it returns and finds the man's heart clean but empty! Then the demon finds seven other spirits more evil than itself, and all enter the man and live in him. And so he is worse off than before." (Matthew 12: 43-45 L.B.)

As our nation moves further and further away from God, so the spiritual hunger increases and false spiritual resources rise up to meet the need. As the movement for renewal in the power of the Holy Spirit increases, so we will see a corresponding increase in the discernment of evil spirits within those who come into His presence in worship or in outreach ministry.

So many hearts are empty! In western countries many people of the last two generations have sought their satisfaction in sexual promiscuity and perversions - in alcohol, drugs, false religious experience, spiritualism and cults. Others have sought comfort or insight into the future by means of superstitious practices or the occult. All these will have left their legacy of evil spirits in many hearts and lives. The desire for satisfaction usually has a root cause: sometimes in social or peer acceptance, or in traumatic emotional situations. Desperation will drive some people to seek answers to life's hurts or simply oblivion; curiosity will provoke others to explore forbidden territory.

Even those who have tasted the mercy, goodness and power of God, can be sorely tempted and fall. God's greatest desire is not that we should have a successful 'ministry' or perform acts of charity or power. Rather he longs to have a growing relationship with each of us. Much depends upon the individual's personal walk with God, the depth of that relationship. If that is lacking or knowingly counterfeited, the person is in great danger. *"Then I will say to them: 'I never knew you. Get away from me you wicked people.'" (Matthew 7:23)*

It is essential in deliverance ministry to have a complementary inner healing ministry. In all the needy situations we have been examining, it is needful to discover the root cause so that an accurate and complete deliverance can be effected. This is not the place to go into the complexities of this ministry, and I am not qualified to do so. Suffice it to say that this process may take a great deal of ministry over several months, especially if the demons have been present a long time and have a stronghold in a tissue of lies.

The person who has entertained demons may well be used to their presence. They are a familiar part of his or her conscious life. The person may not want to part with the security of what they know. Willingness to be delivered is essential even if the person does not fully understand the process. If the original trauma is identified and healed, the outcome is much more likely to be favourable. The minister needs to know their authority in the name of Jesus to bind and cast out the evil spirits, and also be carefully led by the Holy Spirit as to the revealing and timing of the deliverance.

Again, at the conclusion of each session the minister needs to be aware of the danger of leaving a void. The vessel has been emptied or at least partially vacated. Wisdom and compassion dictate that the person who is so affected needs to leave with the knowledge and sense of the Lord's presence, protection and love with them and in them. Without this inner healing they are left bereft and vulnerable. In the conclusion of the story of Saul, we see the dangers of neglecting these guidelines.

Biblical case study
Saul: promising material - too brittle to bend

As we have seen, the Holy Spirit now rested upon David as the anointed one; and Saul was rapidly disintegrating in his personality and as a leader.

"A bruised reed shall He not break." (Isaiah 42:3. A.V.)
A dead tree's branches will be dry and brittle. When the storm comes, they will have no flexibility. In a strong wind they will be resistant and crack and break. A living tree by contrast will have resilience. Its branches will bend to the wind. They may be bruised and bent, but they will not break and they will recover to stand tall and strong. The promise of the Messiah's dealings with us in the Servant Song of *Isaiah 42*, intimate His gentleness and patience with those who have not before understood Him, but who will listen and yield.

It is clear that even at this stage, God was offering Saul opportunities to repent and submit his life and rule to God's greater authority. When the music had touched his inmost being, he could have turned back to God and been delivered. Instead one day he turned on David, even whilst he was playing his harp, and tried to pin him to the wall with his spear. He even turned on his own son, Jonathan, at one point, when he was trying to defend David, and tried to kill him. He demonstrated in his frequent irrational behaviour that he was now a divided person: sometimes giving honour and authority to the anointing of the Holy Spirit, sometimes showing remorse as he recognised his unacceptable behaviour, but at other times allowing aggressive and deceitful evil spirits to control him.

Saul's attitude to David had gone rapidly from affection and gratitude to jealousy and a destructive hatred. He seemed paranoid and consumed with only one aim: to catch the exiled David and kill him. David responded with patience and respect for the king's office. He was assured that God had chosen him to be the next king, and was willing to await God's time for that fulfilment. David's unwillingness to take the opportunities which presented themselves to kill Saul, constantly gave Saul further chances to respond and repent of his jealousy. But this only seemed to enrage the king even more.

"Consult the spirits for me and tell me what is going to happen." (1 Samuel 28:8.) Samuel died and with him Saul's last link with Saul's hope of returning to his

spiritual calling. His final fall from grace and the clearest demonstration of his apostasy came when he broke his own decree. In his fear of the renewed attack by the Philistines, and in his desperation when God did not answer his attempts to consult Him, he finally submitted totally to the evil spirits which were seeking to consume him. He turned to witchcraft and divination, and tried to use a medium to bring up the spirit of the dead Samuel, according to his own perception.

Saul's lack of self-worth had been heavily disguised by his bluster and by his ability to muster followers for battle, but was never revealed for what it was. He could not admit to weakness, so it was not addressed. Jealousy against David revealed his insecurity, but it was too late - there was no going back. It resulted in his lack of trust in God and consequent disobedience. This finally destroyed him, as the manifestation of the apparent spirit of Samuel pointed out. All he gained through the medium was the prophecy of his own death and that of his sons, at the hand of the Philistines—and with it, a crushing despair. (*1 Samuel 28: 19.*)

Saul's final ignominy came when, as his army was defeated by the Philistines, and he was mortally wounded, he begged his weapon-bearer to finish him off so that he wouldn't fall into the hands of the enemy. The young man was too frightened to obey, so Saul then fell on his own sword, effectively committing suicide. The Philistines discovered his corpse and then offered his body to the goddess, Astarte, meaning "shame", of

Philistia. They nailed his headless body to the walls of a garrison town, Beth Shan.

Truly, many more evil spirits had entered this empty house. Saul had started his reign *"among the prophets" (1 Samuel 10:12b N.I.V.)*, but he ended it among the demons.

Notes: Ministry

When taking part in prayer ministry:

1. Deliverance from evil spirits can be affected by any spirit-filled person. God has given us authority over demons. But to be effective, this ministry does require the gift of discernment.
2. If the presence of an evil spirit is suspected within or oppressing someone who has come for prayer for healing, this situation requires careful handling. It may often be preferable to rebuke the evil spirits quietly so as not to alarm the person.
3. Deliverance requires also a discernment of the root cause and has to be completed, as the person may be worse off if they do not experience complete cleansing.
4. It is wise to minister with someone experienced in deliverance as the ministry needs to be accurate, thorough and carefully timed. It may sometimes take a long process of ministry to ensure that the person is completely free.

5. The weaknesses in a person's life, which have allowed the entrance of evil spirits, need to be healed. This is to ensure that the person recognises and repents, and renounces the evil influence.

6. Then in each part of the process of inner healing, there needs to be prayer for healing from the damage inflicted by evil spirits to 'seal up' the spirit against further attack.

Chapter 15
The Disease not the Symptoms

"Where is the dog?" her husband spoke very quietly, almost in a whisper. "In the car" she replied. Minutes before she had been so profoundly deaf that I had to sit right in front of her when I talked so that she could lip-read. We had discerned an emotional problem which we had brought to Jesus and the lady was clearly relieved and joyful. I had moved away from her and had spoken to her in a normal voice. When she replied, it dawned on both of us that the Lord had graciously healed her hearing as well, even though it had not occurred to us to pray for that at the time! I'm sure she had prayed for healing for her hearing many times, and God had honoured her faith. We decided to surprise her husband, and I suggested that he test her with a question she could answer, so he stood behind her to put the question.

I had always seen the ministry of inner healing as separate from other types of healing. That was a false assumption, and it makes our part in the healing process too prominent. We have seen how those persons who are delivered from the effects of demons in their lives need also the ministry of inner healing, both before and after they are set free. It has long been recognised that human nature is composed of body, soul and spirit. We can see these aspects in our experience, but they are not separate. Some physical sicknesses are directly related to, or even caused by, emotional or spiritual pain.

The surface problem might be the direct damage such as that caused by substance abuse or physical assault, for example; but the long-term effects might be much more hidden and serious. We recognise that stress in the mind can cause physical results, such as sleeplessness or stomach ulcers, as toxic chemicals are released into the system. Equally, it is well-known that arthritis often has its origins in bitterness, either on the part of the person suffering it, or by those close to them, as we saw in an earlier situation.

Our personalities are so integrated that God cannot touch one part of our being without affecting another part, as we saw with the man born blind.

If our bodies are healed, our mind and spirit respond in joy and faith. If our spirit is set free, our mind is liberated, and our body is exposed to the healing power of God. So if we minister to the inner person in the area of traumatic memories, we shouldn't be surprised if the body is healed at the same time.

All healing is effected by the Presence of the God who heals. He seeks to make us whole: mind, body and spirit. When we bring someone into that Presence, sometimes there is immediate evidence of His power to heal, but sometimes the person is healed as they go, or sometime later. Some need to return many times for prayer because they could not bear everything to be revealed all at once, or maybe God wants their understanding and cooperation by faith. God seeks always to deepen our relationship with Him.

Sometimes there is a barrier to remove first, before healing can take place, and that is the subject of the next study. *"A man came along who was covered with leprosy. When he saw Jesus he fell with his face to the ground and begged Him: Lord, if you are willing, You can make me clean!" Jesus reached out His hand and..." (Luke 5:12, 13 N.I.V.)* gave him some skin cream! Of course not! Treating the spots would be fruitless. The inner disease would soon regain control.

As we minister we so often try to treat the surface problems. With experience most of us recognise that the problem the person presents with is not the one that most troubles them. The described events and the disturbance on the surface masks the underlying problem. This is often the case when someone asks for prayer for a physical problem. Somehow, it seems that is less shameful than revealing an inner emotional problem. Our wonderful Lord demonstrated how we, by a word of knowledge, can reveal the key to a person's problem and make them whole.

Biblical case study
The paralysed man: a spiritual block

We all experience a form of paralysis at times: physically, mentally or emotionally. We are unable to move, dependent on others, helpless, insecure. Small hindrances in our lives assume major proportions. Sometimes this can be good within a Christian context as it motivates us to receive care from others, and deepens our fellowship. But if it becomes repetitive and morbid, then we need to discern a deeper cause, and seek healing. *"Seeing how much faith they had, Jesus said to the paralysed man: 'My son, your sins are forgiven.'" (Mark 2:5.)* I've always found this story so funny. We have Jesus in a small room crammed with listeners, including some very critical religious types who just want to catch him out. Next the roof is torn open, and I wonder whether the owner of the house was protesting, unheard in the commotion, about this. Four very unorthodox, but very determined, men lower their friend, who is paralysed and helpless, down through the roof gap and lay him right in front of Jesus. We have no record of the man's response to this treatment. Maybe, if he could, he too would have made a protest. He was not able to get there himself, but neither was he able to resist. Anyway, he was carrying a load of guilt, as we shall see. It is very possible he was embarrassed by the whole situation.

His four pals had worked very hard, took the risk of the wrath of the house-owner and ignored the others who were crowding the front door and before them in the queue for healing. (They wouldn't have got away with that in a British queue!) They had allowed nothing to put them off, had exercised immense faith, and now were triumphant. They had made it, Jesus would do His stuff and then all five of them could all go down the pub to celebrate!

Jesus presumably brushed the dust off his robe, and leaned down, pronouncing the words of knowledge and of healing they longed to hear. "What? Sins forgiven? We went through all that struggle to get him here to heal his paralysis, and you, Master, go on about his sin!" They weren't the only ones shocked. The religious leaders saw this as blasphemy—*"God is the only one who can forgive sins!"* (*Mark 2: 6*).

Jesus then spoke His second word of knowledge. He knew their thoughts and He challenged them: *"Is it easier to say to this paralysed man 'Your sins are forgiven' or to say 'Get up, pick up your mat, and walk'"*? (*Mark 2: 9*). Well, which is easier? Most of the modern church would claim that forgiving sins is normal, healing is only exceptional. For Jesus, one followed the other, and both proclaim that the Kingdom of God is among us. Sin in our lives does not frustrate the grace of God, rather the opposite. This man had not said or indicated anything at all. He had not asked for forgiveness or repented, as far as we know. So this was a genuine act of grace.

Sin is not the direct cause of sickness, except when self-inflicted, and even that is not beyond the grace of God. So why did Jesus deal with the hidden sin first? He did not specify what the sin was; indeed He refers to the plural **sins**. He was addressing the spiritual state of the man, the disease of sin. He wanted the man to be an active participant in the healing. The guilt of his sins would have caused him to fear exposure and would have blocked his recognition of Jesus' compassion and power. After all, he was surrounded by disapproving religious leaders.

Jesus might have just been another stuffy religious teacher, ready to condemn and reject him. Instead, the man heard the words of release, of forgiveness, of hope, not just for physical healing, but for his future life. It was then easy for him to believe and to obey Jesus' command, and against all the odds, actually get up and walk out of there. Lack of faith is not usually a primary cause, but a reaction to a deeper problem which renders a person's ability to believe ineffective and powerless.

The most basic message of the ministry of inner healing is that forgiveness is the sum total of inner healing; that is the bottom line. Jesus died on the Cross to remove the curse of sin which resulted in all the ills of the world and of the individual. *"But He was wounded and bruised for our sins. He was chastised that we might have peace; He was lashed --and we were healed!" (Isaiah 53:5 L.B.).* He died that we might be made whole: body, mind and spirit.

Notes: Ministry

When taking part in prayer ministry:

1. Those who minister need to recognise that we are complex, integrated beings, and that the damaged mind, body and spirit of a person are all interrelated
2. We need to be aware that the 'presenting problem' is often not the most urgent or serious.
3. We should not be surprised if, in addressing the physical need for healing, an emotional or

spiritual need is exposed and needs addressing.

4. Again, we should, as we pray for people and bring them into the presence of the Lord, expect to see healing manifest in some or maybe all of these aspects of the damaged person's life, even when we are focussed on one particular aspect. We must not limit the Holy Spirit to our understanding.

5. When we recognise that the root of someone's difficulties is their own sin, even when it is self-inflicted damage, we must be careful to be unshockable and non-judgemental. We always minister grace and mercy.

Chapter 16
Death to Resurrection

"Now if we died with Christ, we believe that we will also live with Him." (Romans 6:8)

There is a precious story told about King George V1. One morning his valet came to bring the king's first cup of tea in his bed-chamber. He knocked on the door, but received no reply. He waited a little then knocked a second time—no sound from within. So the valet tentatively opened the door, and seeing the King kneeling by his bed, in an attitude of prayer, he hastily withdrew. He waited again, and a few minutes later his knock was greeted with a cry "Enter". Once he was inside, the king turned to him, and enquired. "Did you open the door just now?" The servant replied "Yes, sire. Sorry, sire".
The King asked, "And did you see me on my knees?" Even more embarrassed the servant stammered. "Yes, your majesty…" His apology was cut off, for the king said: "If that happens again, please join me—for before **that** King we are all equal."

"What have I done to deserve this?" This is the cry of so many when tragedy strikes. As we saw with the story of the man born blind, it is the wrong question to be asking. Suffering and death are part of everyone's experience. We haven't done anything which brings it on—well not anything exceptional anyway. We all deserve nothing if we are counting up our good deeds, or assessing our faults. It doesn't matter who we are, or what we have done. We are all in the same position before the cross.

For the Christian, though, the answer is quite different. We know we are forgiven and counted completely sin-free in God's sight—but He still has a work to do with us. He doesn't need to find out how much we love Him because He knows the quality of our devotion. He knows our hearts, but we need to know them too. We are often unsure of our sincerity, doubt our commitment and don't know if we have reckoned ourselves dead with Him—until suffering strikes. Then we find out, if we continue to love and serve Him, however much we are hurting and whatever it costs. Then we know that we really meant it. We are privileged if we endure hard trials because God has trusted us with those. He knows we won't give up.

God tailors those trials to our need for healing. He strikes at the heart of the matter as we have seen. God never causes suffering, but, here is a mystery; He sometimes allows it. At other times, He asks us to let go of what is most precious to us. The history of the Christian church is filled with examples of those who have given up what seems to be their special gift - in sport or in academia - to give their lives in serving God, often in very challenging situations. Sometimes, though, God asks us to give up even what we deem His calling and purpose for our lives, for the sake of our healing. *"Now I know that you fear God, because you have not kept back your only son from Him."* (*Genesis 22: 12.*)

Abraham's challenge of sacrificing his son Isaac puts this in focus. (*Genesis 22*).This wasn't a cruel God, asking for human sacrifice to satisfy His lust for blood. He wanted to strengthen Abraham's trust and eradicate his fears. We think of Abraham as this great man of faith who gave up all at the call and left his country and people to travel under God's guidance only to a land he did not know, simply on the promise of God that he would inherit that land and be the father of a great nation, God's chosen people. But as we have seen Abraham three times demonstrated that his faith was not as strong as it appeared, even when he seemed to have a strong relationship with God. (Twice he demonstrated fear and lied about his relationship with his wife Sarah. The third occasion of his faltering faith was when he gave in to Sarah's suggestion and became the father of a substitute son Ishmael).

Now Abraham has triumphed. He has his son of the promise, but God has asked him to sacrifice the very symbol of His faithfulness! Abraham obeys right up to the very brink of the action. His fear has been overcome by trust in the Word of God. *"I have been put to death with Christ on His cross, so that it is no longer I who live, but Christ who lives in me." (Galatians 2:19b-20a)*. That sounds painful, but actually it is a glorious outcome of Christ's healing power. It is often when we are at our very lowest point of loss and despair that God speaks directly into our lives, bringing His balm of healing.

Biblical case study
Mary Magdalene: glorious new life

"Mary (who was called Magdalene) from whom seven demons had been driven out." (Luke 8:2b)

Traditionally the woman, the "sinner", the prostitute, of the story related by Luke in the previous chapter (Luke 7: 36-50) is assumed to be Mary Magdalene, although the identification is complicated, involving any one of three possible women. Even so, she would have at least heard about this story. The woman gate-crashed a Pharisee's party to show her devotion to Jesus by weeping, wetting His feet with her tears, kissing them and anointing them with expensive perfume. Jesus' reflection on this act was to state:
"Therefore I tell you, her sins which were many, have been forgiven; hence she has shown great love." (Luke 7: 47. N.R.S.V.)

Whatever her background, Mary had received a great deliverance from Jesus. It was enough to give her good reason to love Him. We cannot imagine the torment of her previous life, nor the shame and chaos. Now she knew the power of His forgiveness and her response was to become His faithful follower, amongst the other women making provision for His daily needs.

The culmination of her experience of healing was being one of the few disciples who were at the foot of Jesus' cross and heard all His final words: words of forgiveness to His torturers, expressions of care for His mother, His cry of pain to God, *"My God, My God why did You abandon Me?" (Matthew 27:46c).* She would have witnessed the final triumphant cry: *"It is finished." (John 19:30)* Before this, she would have been sick at heart to learn of Jesus' submission to the indignities of the trials before Herod and Pilate. He endured the rejection of the religious elite. His ears were assailed by the mockery of the Jerusalem crowd who screamed for His blood, and the soldiers who plaited the crown of thorns and enrobed Him in purple and jeered that He was the *"King of the Jews".(Mark 15:18b)* Finally there was the scorn of the criminal who was crucified alongside Him. Jesus was exposed as weak and ineffective, portrayed as a malefactor, suffering a murderer's punishment. Much of this she would have appreciated if not completely understood, and yet it would have seared her heart. But her devotion and faith were exemplified in her further actions.

The first person to see Jesus alive was this privileged woman. She had been the first at the tomb on Easter morning, wanting to tend Jesus' broken body, but instead had seen the stone rolled away. She ran to tell the disciples, and after their visit and their strange report that it appeared as if Jesus had passed through His grave clothes, she remained behind at the entrance to the tomb.

She was clearly confused and bewildered by this turn of events. Through her tears she saw two angels in the tomb, but still did not understand. As she turned, Jesus was standing behind her. Maybe because she was blinded by her tears, or because she had her head down in sorrow, she did not recognise Him. Even when He spoke and asked her who she was looking for, she was still in such despair she jumped to the conclusion that He was the gardener.

He only had to say one word, and I can imagine a gentle reproach in the voice. He spoke her name: *"Mary!"* Then she knew Him! *"Master! "* She exclaimed. This was such a simple exchange, but life-changing. *(John 20:16)* Nothing can beat the joyful recognition of Jesus' voice speaking to me, wanting to be reunited with me, showing that He is alive and right there with me. The account says she turned to Him as if to embrace Him, but He did not allow this. She was not to cling to Him because His destiny was to leave His disciples and go back to His Father.

Truly Mary's is a life transformed! Joy must have lent wings to her feet as she returned to report Jesus' resurrection to the other disciples - she whose life had been pulverised by severe demonic oppression, whose self-worth was at rock-bottom until Jesus set her free and allowed her to be one of His closest friends. All this so that Mary now had the dignity of being the sole possessor of the greatest news in world history. Jesus, the Lord, had overcome sin and death and was alive amongst them! *"I am the resurrection and the life."* *(John 11:25a)*

Notes: Ministry

When taking part in prayer ministry:

1. As those who minister, we sometimes have to remember that we are just spectators to what God has been doing in a person's life to bring them to the place they inhabit now. We may have to observe just that and allow Him to continue as we pray for them.
2. Often it is at our lowest ebb Jesus speaks to us. The broken person is the most ready to receive grace and healing.
3. When we meet disappointment, suffering and despair, God can and will minister love, hope and joy through us, often with the simplest of words, or with none at all. Jesus is alive and present whenever we pray. Let Him be who He is!

Chapter 17
Corks and Muddy waters

Have you found some of this uncomfortable or disturbing? Have past events or emotions popped up to the surface of your awareness? If so, think of several corks on the surface of a tub full of water. You can't push them down very easily; you may not have enough fingers. Whilst you are holding one underneath, another may escape. If you do succeed in pushing them down, they will only resurface again once your attention is distracted. It will all be wasted effort and very frustrating!

Or change the image. Think of a muddy pond. The mud accumulated over many years sinks to the bottom. The water seems reasonably clear, until someone stirs up the mud with a stick or their feet. Then the water clouds over with liquid filth. The Holy Spirit is in the business of stirring things up—not just to make us uncomfortable, but to draw our attention to corks or mud in our lives which need to be removed - skimmed off or filtered out. If you are aware of a need for healing, let Him do the work, seek help and prayer from others if you need to. State your need clearly. He will respond to your cry.

If He has revealed something, it is for our cleansing, healing and deep relief. Once we are free of these we feel and look so much more relaxed. Most of all, we experience a renewed sense of how much God loves us and how much trouble He takes over every detail of our lives. Enjoy!

"I ask God from the wealth of His glory to give you power through His Holy Spirit to be strong in your inner selves, and I pray that Christ will make His <u>home</u> in your hearts through faith. I pray that you may have your roots and foundations in love, so that you, together with all God's people, may have the power to understand how broad and long, how high and deep is Christ's love. Yes, may you come to know His love—although it can never be fully known—so become filled with the very nature of God. To Him by whose power working in us is able to do so much more than we can ever ask for, or even think of: to God be the glory in the church and in Christ Jesus for all time, for ever and ever! Amen." (Ephesians 3:16-21)